MW00893059

ALCOHOL IS SH!T

PAUL CHURCHILL

ALCOHOL IS SH!T.
Copyright © 2019 by Paul Churchill.

All rights reserved. Self-published and printed in the United States of America. No part of this book may be used or reproduced in any manner whatsoever without written permission except in the case of brief quotations embodied in critical articles and reviews.

Any digital, electronic or mechanical reproduction or usage, including transmission via internal or external computer network, email, scanning, photo copying, recording or by any other information storing methods, without the written consent from author is strictly prohibited.

Disclaimer
This book contains data, facts and methods about alcohol addiction and treatment that the reader may implement into their life. The author voices that he has no formal training or background and it is highly recommended a reader consult with a medically trained doctor or physician if you decide to quit drinking. Therefore, the author should not be held responsible for any outcomes that may result from implementing strategies mentioned in this book. All facts and sources have been double checked before the publication of this book, but the author cannot guarantee full accuracy of within its first publication.

Some names have been changed to ensure privacy

Edited by Lorca Smetana
Cover design by: Zeljka Kojic

For Information on how to reach the author and Recovery Elevator go to https://www.recoveryelevator.com or email info@recoveryelevator.com.

First Edition
ISBN: 9781086176544

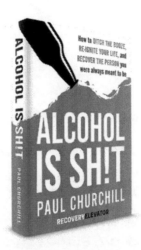

Thank you for purchasing this book.
For a free copy of the audiobook visit
www.recoveryelevator.com/alcoholisshit

10% OF ALL BOOK SALES WILL BE DONATED

TO NON-PROFITS **WHO HELP PEOPLE**

AFFECTED BY ADDICTION

Dedicated to:

Those who find themselves stuck.
To my mom, dad, brother and dog Ben.

Contents

Foreword

I was first introduced to Paul Churchill the same way most of us are: through his podcast Recovery Elevator. It was 2016 and I had quit drinking for exactly 3 days. Not having gone that long without alcohol in years, I thought maybe this would finally be the time to get serious about quitting drinking. I was stuck in a loop where I woke up every morning hungover, full of shame and regret over not being able to stop at one drink the night before like I had intended. I'd make the same promise to myself every morning: today I won't drink. But somehow by 4 p.m., that one glass of wine started to sound really appealing and by 10 p.m. I was near black out again. Sound familiar?

I thought checking out a recovery podcast might help me learn how to drink less, or who knows, maybe not even drink at all. And on that first listen, Paul interviewed a woman who sounded a lot like me. He asked her about those drinking rules you put in the place to try and moderate your alcohol intake (the same rules that I thought were a secret and that I was the only person brilliant enough to use). He asked her the truth about her drinking, about the things she did and thoughts she had, and they were all identical to my daily rituals around alcohol. It suddenly hit me: I wasn't the only person who was struggling with this. That was all it took—I knew I wasn't alone, and something began to shift. I made a decision that night to pursue a life without alcohol. I didn't know exactly how I was going to do it, but I was willing to learn. I created a plan that involved a therapist, 12 Step groups, Paul's Facebook accountability group Cafe RE, and anything else along the way that might help me stop drinking. Three years later, I'm still alcohol free and haven't looked back once.

My friendship with Paul over the last few years has evolved from "that guy who I listen to on the podcast" to "my friend Paul." After being a guest on Recovery Elevator (Episodes 100, 150 and 212), I helped Paul plan his first retreat in Bozeman, Montana, the following summer and we have since become each other's cheerleaders on this path of self-exploration. Cafe RE has been paramount in providing me with a community of support from other people questioning their drinking and I wouldn't be where I am at today without this amazing group of kindred spirits. Paul even helped me get started when I decided to host my own podcast called Recovery Happy Hour. On Recovery Happy Hour I pick up where Paul's guests leave off and we discuss what happens after we get sober, laughing as we dissect the strange and wonderful world of life beyond the bottle.

I've watched newly sober listeners meet Paul for the first time after they've had an experience just like mine, listening to Recovery Elevator and using it as momentum to stop drinking, and when they thank Paul for all that he has done he is usually resistant to accepting any praise. He likes to quickly turn it around and tell them they're the ones who have done all the heavy lifting and he's somewhat correct about that. Paul is more of a catalyst for people's journey in quitting drinking—a precursor to an event where someone undergoes a biological change and a shift in perspective. He helps spark a fire, then they do the work to keep the flames going. Paul has also experienced a more unusual journey than most: one that is public. Since Episode 1 of the Recovery Elevator podcast, Paul has shared his experiences with millions of complete strangers. We've gotten to hear his ups and downs, mistakes and victories, struggles and successes. And throughout the years, his willingness to share his experiences has brought everything from glowing accolades to sharp criticism. But despite the opinions of observers, Paul has made a brave choice to continue to be completely transparent about his journey, always in hopes that someone else might realize they're not alone.

When you first decide to quit drinking, it's easy think it's just about cutting out alcohol. In fact, as you read this book, you may be surprised at how little alcohol is mentioned in the action items. But if you're willing to be open minded and dig into a process of true inner growth—unearthing those reasons why you wanted to drink so much in the first place—you'll begin to realize it's not about the alcohol and it never was. Paul has always seen this path through the lens of optimism and positive thinking: it's not a sacrifice, it's an opportunity. It's not about what you're subtracting from your life, but what you're adding to it.

Alcohol is Shit is a compilation of all that Paul has learned along his journey to living a life that is alcohol free. But make no mistake, this book isn't just about booze. This book is a gentle nudge to learn an entirely new perspective on your life where not only is there no place for alcohol, but no place for habitual, negative thought patterns that are holding you back from living your very best life. If you're reading this book to learn how to quit drinking, the tools are definitely inside. But don't be surprised when you find yourself learning new tools to change other destructive habits, too.

I encourage you to read this book with a pen and a highlighter in hand, to fill the margins with notes, to answer every single one of the Saddle Up questions and to embrace the idea that you won't be able to do this perfectly. This process is messy but beautiful and it's worth embracing with the same kind of fervor you had for drinking. Try not to close your eyes and hold on with a death grip as you experience the ups and downs that a life without alcohol can hand you. This isn't a death sentence, it's an invitation to a new life. So, loosen your grip, let go of your expectations, keep your eyes wide open and enjoy the ride. It's time to uncover who you were meant to be.

Tricia Lewis,
Host of *Recovery Happy Hour*

Introduction

The first thing I'd like to say is congratulations. In fact, this is our very first action item of the book. Put the book down and give yourself a hug. Even if you're in a public place. Tell yourself, "Nice job." Now say it again. Nice job. This book is a celebration of your decision to quit drinking, and please remember this throughout the entire process of reading this book. Fantastic job, because you've listened to your body and you're investing time into yourself to embark upon perhaps the most important journey you'll ever take in life. Sure, this can be challenging, but you've made it further than most by simply showing up and reading this book. Now allow me to personally tell you, nice job! In addition, you're not alone. This path can feel lonely at times, but don't forget I'm with you. You're going to be just fine. Trust me.

First off, I'd like to thank my parents, Molly and Perry, my brother Mark and countless others for helping me get here. It took a lot of hands on deck to get me to a point where I could write this book. I'd also like to thank my Standard Poodle, Ben, who kept me around long enough to quit drinking. There were several moments I didn't think I'd make it, and I even once acted on that thought, but my supportive family, friends and Ben got me through it. Looking back, it all served a purpose and I'm incredibly thankful for the journey. I made it. And so will you.

I knew I had to write this book the moment I said I could never write a book. In June of 2018, I went to a blogging conference in Boise, Idaho where I attended a book writing workshop. Me, write a book? No way. I'm not exactly a wordsmith, which is why I went the podcast route. In fact, in 2011, I misspelled the word "grammar" in a shared calendar at work and I never heard the end of it. It read, "Paul out of office to attend a grammer workshop." No joke.

Fear—we all experience it at some time. Some much more often than others. Part of my motivation in writing this book is to overcome fear, proving to myself I can do this. However, the main point is to talk about the most pressing issue of our time: addiction. This *must* be talked about. Too many people struggle with alcohol, and due to the stigma surrounding addiction, most people reach their most acute moments of pain before reaching out for help, and sometimes, it's too late. I am not okay with this. In this book I will challenge conventional treatment methods, share what worked for me, and provide ideas on how to treat alcoholism and addiction moving forward. Not everyone will agree with these concepts. In fact, some will feel compelled to let me know how they feel, and that's fine. Moving into an alcohol free (AF) life is not black and white, and I intend to cover several different approaches. In this book, I plan to answer the hundreds of questions that listeners have submitted to me over the years. Especially the most critical question, "Do I have a drinking problem or am I an alcoholic…?"

This book will be one-third informational, one-third personal experience and one-third how-to. I've included some of my story for real-life examples of where these concepts unfolded in my journey. Of course, I'd like to think my story is special, or unique, but it's not. Everyone's story has different details, dates and locations, but after interviewing over 250 people on the Recovery Elevator podcast, most stories are strikingly similar. Having said that, from this moment on, I want you to focus on the similarities and not the differences. The mind will do its best to convince you that you don't have anything in common with a guy who has a Standard Poodle named Ben and whose favorite band is Third Eye Blind. Be aware of this trap that the mind can set.

Let's cover some basics on how to read this book. First piece of advice: relax. Nothing is under control and that's a good thing. Take your control throttle from level ten and gently ease it down a few gears. If you let it, the body will do most of the healing and work during this journey. It will tell you exactly what to do. It already has—you're reading this book. This may sound strange, but you can't think yourself out of this predicament, because you're relying on the same brain that thought yourself into this dilemma. I know, it's a mind fuck, but stick with me. I should, fingers crossed, be able to tie this all together in the coming pages.

Do not, at any moment while reading this book, take yourself too seriously. Smiles and laughter are powerful tools in this journey, which is why I will be starting off each chapter with a "you might need to ditch the booze if…" line. It's imperative that you make room for smiles and create lightheartedness.

It's also crucial that you be willing to step outside your comfort zone during the reading of this book. You've already flexed those muscles by picking it up. Nice job. I can assure you, the amazing life that awaits is located outside of your comfort zone. I stepped outside my comfort zone when I quit drinking on September 7th, 2014, and then catapulted myself even further outside the comfort zone when I launched the Recovery Elevator podcast on February 25th, 2015. It was not easy. I had trouble sleeping for three months after I launched the podcast. I would lay awake at night and say, "Oh fuck, what have I done? I just came out to the world about my struggles with alcohol." I didn't know it at the time, but that was the best decision I could have made.

For some, this may be a challenge. For others, not as much and it can even be enjoyable. For some, the word "challenge" may be the understatement of a lifetime, but as I mentioned earlier, this is most important journey you'll ever embark upon so no matter how hard it gets, I want you to promise me you won't quit. And most likely, the hardest part, the emotional muck that alcohol dragged you through is already behind you.

This book may stir up unpleasant feelings. The most powerful pharmacy on the planet is found in your brain and at times, it may kick up uncomfortable emotions trying to convince you that an AF life isn't what the doctor ordered. I'll show you how to use this pharmacy in your favor. While reading this book, do me a favor and don't attach yourself to an emotion, label, identity or outcome. I'm not lying when I say an incredible life awaits you, but at this moment, I want you to be present here and now.

You're going to read some unnerving stats about alcohol and addiction. The point is to inform, and not motivate you to make changes based on fear. Fear-based changes, which are always made on willpower, don't last long.

In this book, you'll slowly start to get memos past the analytical part of the brain to the subconscious part that runs 95% of the show.

I encourage you to reread this book when you're at a different spot in your journey. You may be reading this during the "Dr. Google" information collecting phase, or you may be approaching Zen master level 10 status with ample time beyond your last drink. Wherever you are is right where you need to be, which is right here in this moment.

By simply reading this book, you will become more knowledgeable about alcohol, addiction, and how to quit drinking, but I strongly recommend you "saddle up" and explore the action items at the end of the chapters and segments. Read this book with a friend and work through the "saddle up" discussions and actions items together. I encourage you to read this book with a notebook, pen and highlighter. Perhaps even with a box of tissues nearby. You may purge emotions while reading this book and you should begin to feel lighter the further you read. What you get out of this book will mirror the level of attention and effort you put into it.

While reading, you'll encounter the phrase "normal drinker"—someone who doesn't struggle with alcohol. Now keep in mind, the distinction between a normal drinker and someone addicted to alcohol is foggy. In fact, I'm not fully convinced there is such thing as a normal drinker. It just depends where you currently are on the risk scale, which I'll describe later.

Don't worry about the word alcoholic. I've officially broken up with the word several times. I've done it officially on the podcast twice: Episodes 75 and 159. I feel the word alcoholic fuels the stigma surrounding alcoholism, and a focal point of writing this book is to help eradicate the stereotypes this label carries. Of course, when attending a 12 Step meeting I say, "Hi, my name is Paul, I'm an alcoholic," out of respect for the program, and I may refer to myself or someone else in this book as an alcoholic, but I think it's time we start using a new set of words to describe addiction and recovery. I'll be using the word alcoholism to reference the disease of addiction (I'll address the disease model later). You'll also encounter the acronym AUD, which stands for alcohol use disorder. I also reference someone who struggles with alcohol as someone with enhanced dopamine receptors or EDR.

Who am I? Let me be clear. I'm not a doctor, therapist, psychologist, psychiatrist, clinician, dietician, respiratory therapist, biomedical scientist, oncologist, or paranormal investigator. I'm just a guy with a giant red poodle who listened to his body and quit drinking the most dangerous drug on the planet: alcohol. I became curious about what addiction is and how to move forward in life without alcohol. I started doing research and interviewing people who had also quit drinking. My goal in this book is to share everything I've learned with the reader and to empower you on this journey. I've yet to meet someone who is too far gone. Not even close. Everyone has the capacity to ditch the booze and heal parts of the personality that resorts to alcohol when life gets cumbersome.

I want this book to be lighthearted and fun, but I also want it to be real. Addiction is a bitch… and can be a matter of life and death. We aren't truly living while under the influence and we certainly aren't living life to the fullest when numbed by alcohol. This book isn't about staying away from alcohol but returning to a joyful life where alcohol is no longer needed. Where we can authentically be present and enjoy social situations without a cocktail in our hands.

This book, like all, has a beginning and an end, but they aren't located in the customary locations.

You may have recently gone through unpleasant times in life (thank you, alcohol), but I want to remind you that planes take off in the wind. And you're about to take off.

Saddle up

☐ Give yourself a hug, pat yourself on the back, and tell yourself nice job for reading this book. Remind yourself you have the courage to continue reading and to explore a life without alcohol. This isn't punishment, but a celebration of a new chapter in life.

☐ Remind yourself again and again—you're not alone.

☐ While reading this book, do your best to focus on the similarities and not the differences.

☐ For five minutes, close your eyes and envision a life where alcohol is no longer needed. A life filled with warmth, compassion, love, wholeness and whatever your heart desires.

Chapter 1
What is Addiction?

*"**You might need to ditch the booze if...**you go on Nutrisystem not to lose weight, but because you are always too drunk or hung over to cook for yourself."*

—Jonathan, Gilbert, AZ

Where does it come from? How does it start? Can it be overcome? I'll address the last question right now and say absolutely. Yes, it can, and I'll show you how in this book, but first we need to understand what addiction is. First off, addiction is complicated. Addiction stems from biological, chemical, connection, emotional, social, political, economic, genetic, and environmental components. I think it was around Episode 100 of the Recovery Elevator podcast when I humbly admitted to myself, "Fuck, addiction is confusing."

Describing addiction in words is difficult. The Romans used the word addictus, which referred to someone who, having defaulted on a debt, was assigned to his creditors as a slave—hence, enslavement to a habit. For someone who has struggled with addiction, no definition or explanation is needed; for a normal drinker, no amount of explanation will suffice. Addiction is puzzling, riddled with paradoxes and most medical professionals aren't equipped with the knowledge or tools to treat addiction. To make matters worse, an addiction often takes hold long before the host is aware of it.

In the words of a consensus statement by addiction experts in 2001, addiction is a chronic neurobiological disease, characterized by behaviors that include one or more of the following: impaired control over drug use (alcohol), compulsive use, continued use despite harm and cravings.

According to addiction guru and specialist Dr. Gabor Mate, on the biochemical level the purpose of addiction is to create an altered physiological state in the brain. He also says that addiction is never purely psychological and that all addictions have a biological dimension as well. Addictions form when we resort to regulating our internal states with external substances.

In this book we will be focusing on the addiction to alcohol but there are countless more, such as sex, gambling, food, exercise, shopping, social media, suffering, and thinking, to name a few. In addition, addiction is repeated use of a substance with continued negative consequences, and these users can never be fully satiated. I gave this theory the ultimate field test with alcohol for about a decade. It didn't go well. When two sex addicts finally meet, one might say, "Problem solved," but that isn't actually the case. Addiction is uncontrollable mental time travel to the past and future and we temporarily ground ourselves in the present with alcohol. I also feel addiction is a reflection of the current state of society.

Where does addiction come from? According to Eckhart Tolle, "Every addiction arises from an unconscious refusal to face and move through your own pain. Every addiction starts and ends in pain. You're using someone or something to cover up the pain." Pema Chodron says that addiction arises when the edge of life is too sharp.

When I first began the Recovery Elevator podcast, I felt that alcoholism was 80% genetic and about 20% environmental. Today, I've taken a reverse stance. We are a traumatized society and you don't need to serve in Afghanistan or Iraq to experience this. According to *The Body Keeps the Score* by Bessel van der Kolk, one in five Americans was sexually molested as a child. One in four was beaten by a parent to the point where it left a mark. One in three couples engage in physical violence. One in four grew up with an alcoholic relative and one in eight witnessed their parents being hit. Fortunately, I didn't experience any of these traumas (thank you, Mom and Dad), but much of my pain came from loneliness. I grew up in Salt Lake City, Utah, where I was one of only a handful of non-Mormons in school. There were times when classmates told me I wasn't invited to their birthday parties because I wasn't Mormon. Or the reason why I didn't get a Valentine card was because I didn't attend their church. I remember in the 2nd grade I was told I was going to hell because of my faith. My mom once witnessed a similar dialogue take place at a public swimming pool between me and another kid. Wow, did she step in and let this kid have it! In the first twelve years of my life, I felt as if I didn't belong. Then, luckily, my dad was laid off and we moved to Vail, Colorado when I was in the seventh grade. I was a normal drinker until I had my heart broken at the age of 21. While studying abroad in Spain, I fell in love with a Dutch girl. I returned to America and she to Holland. When I say heartbroken, I mean 54 trillion little pieces. The pain and loneliness were unbearable, and I remember one night in the summer of 2003, after working parking lot duty at the Orange County fair (worst job ever), I bought a 6-pack of Michelob Ultra and the pain seemed to subside. This was the night my addiction to alcohol began. I want to be clear; I don't blame anyone for this, including myself. My addiction to alcohol wasn't the result of Mormons, my family, or a Dutch girl. It's just how it went, and I wouldn't change a thing because this path led me to an incredible life and the same can happen with you.

My experience with addiction mirrors the definitions above. I wanted to depart from the present moment where my loneliness lived, and alcohol was the magical elixir. I feel my addiction to alcohol was mostly environmental, but I'm sure there was some genetic factor at play. I like the analogy that genetics loads the gun and the environment pulls the trigger.

A common narrative with my podcast interviewees and my own personal experience is that the first drink produced a "wow" factor like none other. These are some of the responses to their first drinks. "Oh my god, this is it." "This is what I've been missing my whole life." "Game on." "I finally belong." "Giddy up." "You (alcohol) and me are going to be best friends." I remember my first drink at the age of thirteen produced a similar euphoric feeling and I couldn't get enough. Well, my body said it had enough when I projectile vomited on my friend's basement floor. I've asked over 100 normal drinkers what their experiences were when they took the first drink and the responses were: "Tasted like shit," "I guess it was okay," "It didn't really do much for me," "What's all the hype about," "I don't get it." Clearly not everyone has the same experience after taking their first drink. Is there a gene or a genetic predisposition at play?

Despite the discovery of DNA in 1860 and uncovering the structure in the 1950s, scientists have yet to discover the gene for addiction and I don't think they will. There is research showing that alcoholics have a genetic mutation with the A1 allele gene causing them to metabolize dopamine differently, but this is observed after chronic drinking has already taken place. According to Dr. Jaak Panksepp, in *affective neuroscience,* the view that genes play a decisive role in the way a person's brain develops has been replaced by a radically different notion; the expression of genetic potential is, for the most part, contingent on environment. The new and exciting science of epigenetics has basically torched the old-school idea that your genes are your destiny. It's the environment that signals the body to turn on and off certain genes. If one or both parents are alcoholics, this doesn't indicate a child will suffer from alcoholism. Remember, there isn't a gene specific to addiction. According to recent research, brain development in the uterus and in childhood is the single most important biological factor in determining whether a person will be predisposed to addiction. Dr. Vincent Felitti, chief investigator in a landmark study of over seventeen thousand middle-class Americans said, "The basic cause of addiction is predominantly experience-dependent during childhood and not substance dependent."

To explore addiction further, our path will lead us to dopamine which is a key brain chemical messenger. Dopamine isn't a pleasure molecule, but a learning molecule and a key player in the reward system in our brain. It is known that alcohol reduces the inhibition of dopamine releasing cells, but again, this occurrence is after the fact. Do all human beings experience sensations, tastes, smells, sights, sex, and alcohol the same? The answer is no. Some of us have more sensitive dopamine receptors than others. This is an evolutionary trait that was key to human survival. It made some walk just a little further to find food, to find the warmth of fire and to find a mate. People with these enhanced dopamine receptors (EDRs) experience things differently, including alcohol. Having these enhanced dopamine receptors was a tremendous asset for the evolution of humans but ironically in modern times, it can backfire. This reward system, which isn't much different in rats, is a primitive part of the brain and exists to ensure we seek what we need in order to stay alive. It alerts us to sights, sounds and smells that point us in the right direction. Operating in the realm of instinct, it was built for when survival depended on the ability to obtain food and sex before the competition arrived. This is an incredible system, but it can trip us up in a modern world with opportunities 24/7 to fulfill our desires. In my opinion, an addiction occurs when people with EDRs experience trauma and they seek to soothe this inner pain with the external substance alcohol.

Is addiction a disease?

In 1956, the American Medical Association classified addiction as a disease. According to National Geographic Magazine in the September 2017 issue, addiction causes hundreds of changes in brain anatomy, chemistry and cell-to-cell signaling, including the gaps between neurons called synapses which are the molecular machinery for learning. By taking advantage of the brain's marvelous plasticity, alcohol addiction remolds neural circuits to assign supreme value to alcohol, at the expense of other interests such as health, work, family or life itself. Dr. Antonello Bonci, a neurologist at the National Institute on Drug Abuse says, "In a sense, addiction is a pathological form of learning." In the part of the cerebral cortex responsible for regulating emotional impulses and for making rational decisions, alcohol-addicted brains have reduced activity. This is why there are so many incredible YouTube videos of drunk people doing stupid shit. After my first year of college, four friends and I, while drunk, decided it would be a good idea to steal a trashcan full of range balls from the local golf course. After loading 5,000 golf balls into the car, we thought it would it would be fun to throw the balls onto the street while driving back to my house. Well, the next day when the golf course realized they had zero golf balls for golfers to hit, all they had to do was follow the bread crumbs of golf balls to my parents' house. My mom was SO pissed. The local newspapers did a good job of covering how alcohol makes people do stupid shit when they did a feature story on us. You can imagine how awkward we felt doing 100 hours of community service at the very same golf course. Fuck, that was embarrassing.

Although there is still much to learn about what addiction is, the medical community is moving forward in the right direction. If you had opened a medical textbook 30 years ago, it would have declared that addiction is the dependence on a substance with increasing tolerance, requiring more and more to feel the same effects. Then you insert nasty withdrawal when the substance is removed. The old model also doesn't address perhaps the most treacherous part of addiction, which is relapse and why people go back to drinking after the body is no longer physically dependent. This older description doesn't explain why someone with years away from drinking alcohol picked up a drink again, despite having a good indication of what will happen. This antiquated model came with an ineffective solution of punishing or incarcerating addiction out of people. Individuals often internally implement this strategy with intense self-loathing... does this sound familiar?

Nowadays, the great majority of the medical community recognizes addiction/alcoholism as a disease, and they are all starting to sing the same tune. Just as with any other disease, treatment for addiction needs to come with compassion, love, and the understanding it isn't the fault of the drinker.

Addiction isn't a weakness of character or a moral failing and most medical professionals as well as the general public are coming around as well, recognizing that no one ought to punish or blame the person suffering with addiction. After all, no one blames someone who has cancer, multiple sclerosis or diabetes. In the late 1970s and early 1980s in America, a more compassionate view of addiction started to emerge.

Public figures such as former astronaut Buzz Aldrin were beginning to speak out with their struggles with addiction. Then the tough love "Just Say No" campaign was implemented by the Reagan administration and we took a few steps back. However, after a couple of decades of trying to incarcerate and shame addiction out of people, we're recognizing that that strategy isn't working, and we're moving towards more compassionate treatment methods.

What do I think about the disease model? Sure, after years of drinking there are visible neurological changes in the addicted brain that can be observed in a brain scan, but I don't fully subscribe to the disease model by itself and it doesn't explain why the addiction took hold in the first place. I feel addiction stems from other causes that science cannot quantify, such as past traumas, a lack of emotional support in adolescence, an internal disconnection, enhanced dopamine receptors, false marketing campaigns from Big Alcohol, and more. I personally won't be telling my subconscious that I have a chronic brain condition that I'll have to grapple with for the rest of my life. I feel that alcoholism and addictions are indicators that a change needs to happen, and that we can fully right the ship in life. It's important to believe that the intense suffering you've experienced with alcohol will be the catalyst that propels you into a happier life, rather than something that gave you a chronic brain condition. The body and mind together have the capacity to fully heal itself. Trust me, I've met thousands of people in rough shape who have fully unfucked themselves. You can too.

A common misperception is that addictive substances such as alcohol, cocaine, meth, and heroin, to list a few, are the main drivers of addiction. That once a user tries an addictive drug such as heroin or cocaine for example, they will instantly become addicted, but this isn't the truth. A study shows that less than 2% of users who try cocaine become addicted, and many users only try the drug once. If addictive molecular structures were the sole culprits of creating addiction, narcotics for pain relief wouldn't be offered at all. Medical evidence continues to show that opioids prescribed for pain management, even for longer periods of time, do not lead to addiction except for in a small minority of people. Gambling can be a destructive addiction without anyone stating that society needs to get rid of dice. According to Lance Dodes, a psychiatrist at the Harvard Medical School Division on Addictions and author of *The Sober Truth*, "Addiction is a human problem that resides in people, not in the drug or the drug's capacity to produce physical effects." In the TED Talk titled the "Opposite of Addiction is Connection" by Johan Hari—which I highly recommend watching—he talks about how addiction is much more than an addictive drug and that if we address the environment, the internal disconnection can heal.

Despite popular belief, only a handful of people who try opiates become addicted. The U.S. Government thought it had a huge problem on its hands when they realized that nearly 20% of their soldiers in Vietnam during the late 1960s and early 1970s were using heroin. They began preparing for the return of nearly 500,000 addicted soldiers. However, what happened after the soldiers returned from the war surprised authorities. The remission rate was at 95% and most soldiers simply stopped using these drugs.

Why did U.S. soldiers who were using heroin in Vietnam discontinue use of these addictive drugs after they returned from service? Why were they able to stop, most without any formal treatment or support at all, despite the common belief that heroin is the most dangerous and addictive drug on the planet? (I will cover what is the most dangerous drug on the planet shortly.)

Dr. Bruce Alexander, a psychologist at Simon Fraser University in British Colombia, set out to answer this question. Laboratory animals, in this instance, rats, can be coerced into addiction by altering their environments. Dr. Alexander set up an environment where one rat in a cage by itself had unlimited access to water and to another dispenser which contained water infused with cocaine. The rat was able to administer the water or cocaine at any time with a lever system. What he found was that it was only a matter of time before the rat ended up killing itself by drinking strictly from the water infused with cocaine. Dr. Alexander then conducted a similar experiment he called Rat Park. Rat Park was spacious, with about 200 times the amount of space as a typical laboratory cage. It was also scenic, with a peaceful British Columbia forest painted on the walls and comfortable, with ample lounging areas for hanging out. This environment was also sociable, with 16-20 rats of both sexes. In addition, there were tunnels, swings, wheels, slides and a 65" HD flat screen with Netflix playing reruns of "It's Always Sunny in Philadelphia" (such a great show). I'm kidding, there wasn't Netflix, but you get the point. This was an oasis for rats. Also, in Rat Park the rats could release a fluid from either of two drop dispensers. One dispenser contained a morphine solution and the other an inert solution.

Unlike for the lone rat in a small cage, the morphine held little attraction, even when it was dissolved in a super-sweet liquid which is usually irresistible to rodents. This occurred even after the rats were forced to consume morphine the weeks before being placed into Rat Park to the point where the rats experienced uncomfortable withdrawal symptoms. They found that caged rats consume up to twenty times more morphine than their contemporaries did in Rat Park. You might be saying, "Cool, Paul, but these are rats," but keep in mind that the dopamine reward system in rats is eerily like the dopamine system in humans. We also witnessed a real-life Rat Park with the soldiers in Vietnam upon their return home. Portugal also witnessed this as they drastically changed the environment towards addiction in 2001 when they decriminalized nearly all drugs and placed those resources towards helping addicts and not putting them in institutions.

I feel a few critical components need to occur for an addiction to take hold. A current or past environment filled with stress, trauma, loneliness, or abandonment, to name a few, along with enhanced dopamine receptors, and an addictive drug. If you're reading this book, that drug was most likely alcohol.

Saddle up

☐ Tell yourself, preferably while looking at yourself in the mirror, that addiction is not a weakness of character or a moral failing.

☐ List a few things you've done while drinking that you wouldn't have done otherwise.

☐ Can you think of any past traumas that happened in childhood or other periods in your life? This can also include things that didn't happen, such as a lack of love and emotional support.

☐ Regarding the definitions of addiction you've read above, can you think of other substances, people, behaviors, actions or thoughts you might be addicted to?

☐ Write down what your first experience with alcohol was like. Do you think enhanced dopamine receptors played a role? Did you continue to chase that feeling?

☐ Write down your own definition of addiction and how it has progressed and taken hold in your life.

☐ Ask yourself if you agree with the disease model. Do you think addiction is genetic?

☐ Do you agree with Rat Park model? Are you living in an environment that cultivates wholeness? If not, what do you think needs to change?

☐ How do you think society should handle addiction?

Chapter 2
Alcohol: The Spirit and Drug

"You might need to ditch the booze if...you blame your hangovers on not knowing how much wine you're drinking because it's out of a giant box."

—Amber, Arroyo Grande, CA

First off, alcohol is shit. It kills over three million people worldwide each year, over 88,000 in the US alone, and kills more people each year than every other drug combined. Yikes.

Alcohol is undeniably pure shit.

- Someone dies from alcohol every ten seconds.
- Alcohol doesn't make you forget anything—when you're "blacked out," the brain temporarily loses the ability to create memories.
- Alcohol poisoning kills six Americans each day.
- 31% of rock stars' deaths are due to alcohol.
- Rumor has it, Alexander the Great once held a drinking contest and when it was over, 42 of his soldiers had perished. Oops.
- A century ago, men were three times more likely to have a problem with alcohol. Today, the odds for men and women are about the same.
- According to the first ever U.S. surgeon general's report released in November of 2016, 21 million Americans struggle with addiction, making this a more prolific problem than cancer.
- Even Noah, who built a giant wood boat and stuffed it to the brim with animals, had a rough time with alcohol. According to

the Bible, Noah drank wine and he lay unconscious in his test which then caused difficulties with his family.

- Alcohol kills someone every ten seconds worldwide.
- Alcohol is involved in nearly 50% of all domestic violence incidents and violent crimes.
- In 2012, 5.9% of all global deaths were attributable to alcohol consumption.
- Alcohol and alcohol-related problems drain nearly 200 billion dollars from the U.S. economy each year.
- Alcohol is involved in roughly 55% of adult drownings.
- Alcoholics are sixteen times more likely than others to die in falls and ten times more likely to become burn victims.
- In 40% of all fatal pedestrian accidents, the driver, pedestrian, or both were intoxicated.
- It is estimated that 40% of hospital beds are occupied due to alcohol-related issues.

Alcohol can wreak havoc on us spiritually, mentally, and physically. The word alcohol is said to come from the Arabic term "al-khul" which literally means "body-eating spirit" or "demon." Let that sink in for a moment. Alcohol is a spirit. In several societies it's called "spirits." We drink this spirit in hopes of rising above thinking, to quiet the mind, but eventually it takes us to an unconscious level where the spirit alcohol takes over. Alcohol… you sneaky son of a gun!

In the words of writer and health enthusiast Jason Christoff, "In alchemy, alcohol is used to extract the soul essence of an entity. Hence its use in extracting essences for essential oils, and the sterilization of medical instruments. By consuming alcohol into the body, it in effect extracts the very essence of the soul, allowing the body to be more susceptible to neighboring entities, most of which are of low frequencies." This sounds about right. While owning and operating a bar in Spain, I nearly lost my soul…. and I'm not kidding.

The first victim of this life-extraction process is yeast, which dies during the process of making alcohol. The second, as is the case with many, is the joy and life energy of the consumer.

This snippet sums it up perfectly.

I drank for happiness and became unhappy
I drank for joy and became miserable
I drank for sociability and became argumentative
I drank for sophistication and became obnoxious
I drank for friendships and became enemies
I drank for sleep and woke up tired
I drank for strength and felt weak
I drank for relaxation and got the shakes
I drank for courage and became afraid
I drank for confidence and became doubtful
I drank to make conversation easier and slurred my speech
I drank to feel heavenly and ended up feeling like hell.

—Author unknown

Yep, alcohol has climbed to the top of the shit list.

The drug alcohol

I don't want to get too in-depth with how alcohol interacts with the body and mind, but I do want to cover the basics. The following paragraphs are intended to inform, debunk myths, and briefly cover how alcohol interacts with the body and mind. Don't worry about memorizing or writing any of this down. My goal is to inform and not to motivate you to quit drinking based on fear, because that approach is never sustainable in the long run.

The drug alcohol can easily be argued as the most dangerous drug on the planet. Alcohol is ethanol with a couple of additives added to it to make it palatable and tolerable for humans to consume. It's a simple chemical with complex effects on the body and mind. What is alcohol? Yeast shit (back to the book title). When yeast, a microorganism that evolved over two hundred million years ago, encounters the water and plant sugars in fruits, berries and grains, the process of fermentation occurs. Yeast then releases an enzyme that converts sugars into carbon dioxide and ethanol. This newly created simple chemical, once ingested, then changes several more times and eventually the chemical structure resembles another addictive chemical compound that is currently derailing society: opiates.

Alcohol acts on several parts of the brain, and some argue it's a more complex drug than heroin and cocaine, which target just one area of the brain. Alcohol spikes the amount of gamma-aminobutyric acid (GABA), which slows down activity in the central nervous system and decreases the flow of glutamate which activates the nervous system. This is the primary reason why alcohol can make you temporarily feel more relaxed and worry less. Alcohol also cues the brain to release dopamine, the pleasure/learning molecule.

In time, the brain adjusts to excess alcohol consumption and begins to produce less GABA and more glutamate resulting in anxiety, depression and overall discontent. These are also the contributing factors to the new term "hangxiety," which is intense anxiety after a heavy night of drinking and is the fucking worst. As if this wasn't enough, dopamine production slows, and the consumer will eventually experience less pleasure out of everyday activities. Within time, these progressive changes lead us to a critical point: we drink to avoid feeling bad instead of drinking to feel good. I experienced this shift in 2006 during the second year of owning the bar in Spain. Reaching this tipping point isn't fun, and it's around this time when we start to question the role alcohol is playing in our life.

In addition, when present in the brain, alcohol causes the prefrontal cortex to operate like a faulty pinball machine; the flippers work, but the score doesn't add up properly. The prefrontal cortex is responsible for rational thought and pragmatism and when this system is compromised with alcohol, insert Murphy's Law.

In low doses (1-2 drinks), alcohol is a stimulant, increasing blood flow, accelerating the heart rate and speeding up the transmission of nerve impulses. With two or more drinks, alcohol become a depressant/sedative. People often mistake this as the calming or relaxing effect of alcohol, but in reality, parts of your brain and faculties are beginning to shut down. Your thoughts slow, logic says, "Peace, I'm out," speech starts to slur, it becomes difficult to connect thoughts, and your memory starts to experience gaps or blackouts. "Alcohol does not make us do things better; it just makes us less ashamed of doing them badly," noted Sir William Osler (1849-1919), a physician and professor of medicine at the Johns Hopkins School of Medicine.

To complicate matters more, alcohol causes blood sugar levels to go haywire. Even if you consume sugar-free alcoholic drinks, the alcohol cues production of the hormone epinephrine (adrenaline) which sends a message to the liver to start breaking down glycogen into glucose, which can then result in hypoglycemia. Even in the short term, since glucose is the brain's most important readily available source of energy, when we stop drinking we are likely to experience irritability, intense emotions, mood swings, fatigue, mental confusion, intense anxiety, and panic attacks. Again, anxiety is the WORST and was a catalyst for why I quit drinking. This explains why it's common to have intense sugar cravings in the subsequent months after we quit drinking. I think I breached the 500,000 Reece's Pieces mark in my first 60 days.

The Metabolism of Alcohol— In Case You'd Like to Know

Five to ten percent of the of alcohol you drink is absorbed into the bloodstream through the lining of the mouth and esophagus. Then about 20% is absorbed into the bloodstream through the stomach and the remaining 70-75% through the walls of the small intestines.

In the first step of eliminating alcohol from your system, alcohol is converted into acetaldehyde, and the second step involves the liver creating the enzyme aldehyde dehydrogenase (ADH) to finish the job. Things start to go south when we overburden this system which is why the amazing human body has a backup system called the microsomal enzyme oxidizing system (MEOS). When larger quantities of alcohol are consumed, the MEOS system kicks in to help with the overflow. Six-plus drinks in a night? No problem. The body says, "get in the game MEOS." This is typically what happens when we binge drink, which is defined by the NIAAA (National Institute of Alcohol Abuse and Alcoholism) as four drinks for women and five drinks for men over a span of two hours. The problem is that once the MEOS system clocks in, it doesn't want to clock out. Since this backup system quickly and efficiently metabolizes alcohol, the result is me being able to drink nearly twice as much as my friends. Or as interviewee David says in Episode 142 of the podcast, he found himself continuously lapping the pace car. This is why some drinkers develop a higher tolerance for alcohol, and once it's activated, it's tough to tell the MEOS system to take a seat. Because of this, if we quit drinking for a while and then begin drinking again, we will pick up right where we left off.

Another reason alcohol can make us feel like total dog doodoo is that it jumps the queue for metabolism in the liver. The body accurately tags alcohol as a "level 10 toxin" and says, "Let's get rid of this shit ASAP." Meanwhile, other calories and toxins that your body is still working to expel have to wait in line before getting filtered out. A couple things can happen if this process continues: 1. The liver says "Hey, I hope you're enjoying the party because we can't get rid of the shit fast enough," and the C word (in this book it means cirrhosis) starts to develop and 2. All the other toxins that normally are removed from the body through the liver start to build up and can cause other diseases. Both options are no bueno.

Earlier I mention acetaldehyde which is a byproduct of the digestion of alcohol. Once enough acetaldehyde builds up in the system (and binge drinking is the biggest culprit of this) a new generation of chemical is created called tetrahydroisoquinolines (TIQs). Once an excess of TIQs are floating around the body, they find their final resting place in the brain where they can permanently accumulate. Abnormal amounts of TIQs in the brain can stimulate, upon the first drink, an abnormal intake of alcohol. This buildup of TIQs is the brain is the reason we find it harder and harder to stop drinking once we start. And this is why despite telling ourselves we'll have just one or two, we end up having much more. The problem isn't the last drink, it's the first.

Despite the MEOS staying in the "on" position and the potential buildup of TIQs, thanks to neuroplasticity, the brain and body can fully recover. Trust me. I often get asked the question if a person can be "too far gone," and the answer is no. I've yet to meet someone who hasn't been able to successfully say "sayonara" to alcohol. We arrive on this planet with all the tools necessary for the body and mind to repair themselves. We'll cover countless techniques in the following chapters of how to do this, but first we need to decide if this is the right journey for you…

Great job. You're doing fantastic. Set this book down for a moment and take three deep breaths. Ready, go.

Saddle up

- ☐ Do you agree that alcohol is a drug? Does it have a spirit?
- ☐ Ask yourself what you drank for and if it was delivered.
- ☐ As your drinking progressed, did you experience less pleasure from day-to-day activities? What are some specific activities you used to enjoy more?
- ☐ Do you drink to feel good or to avoid feeling bad?
- ☐ Do you find it harder than it used to be to stop drinking once you've started?
- ☐ Have you ever taken time off from alcohol and then were surprised at how fast it ramped up again?
- ☐ Take three deep breaths. Inhale for several seconds and then exhale for several seconds.

Chapter 3
The Million Dollar Question:
"Do I Have a Drinking Problem?"

"You might need to ditch the booze if...... the first
thing you do upon seeing your car in the impound lot after
crashing it drunk is grab the unopened Lime-a-Ritas and tall
boys in the back seat (then cry.)"

—Blair, Omaha, NE

Do I have a drinking problem? Do I have an alcohol use disorder? Do I have enhanced dopamine receptors? Is my relationship with alcohol unhealthy? Do I need to take a break from alcohol for a few days, weeks, months or possibly the rest of my life???? Am I drinking more because my job is becoming more stressful? And do I dare ask this question, am I, um, an…alcoholic?

I'm sure part of you has made a compelling case that alcohol is benign and hasn't been holding you back in life. Do any of these lines sound familiar?

- I did a 30-day challenge so surely, I can't have a problem, right?
- I can attend social events without drinking so I assume alcohol isn't an issue.
- I've never had a traffic violation involving alcohol, I haven't been fired from a job, nobody has ever told me I drink too much or that I should even cut down on my drinking.
- I don't drink in the mornings; I don't drink if I have work obligations and I refuse to drink alone.
- I can easily go a few days or weeks without alcohol.

- I'm in my 30s. I'm way too young to have a drinking problem, right?
- I highly doubt I have a drinking problem because I ran two half marathons last year and I go to the gym nearly every day.
- I drink as much as my friends do; this is normal.
- When I do drink, the next day I might feel a little "off," but I've never needed a drink to steady shaky hands.

I'm guessing that, for the majority of readers, this is why you're reading this book: to assess your drinking. To determine if alcohol should be removed from your diet... or not. To find out if you need to make what will perhaps be the biggest change in your life. For a handful of lucky readers, this question may have already been answered. For others, we're still trying to answer the million-dollar question.

For many of us, this can be the most difficult question we address in life. I know it was for me. Many, including myself, seek guidance from physicians, therapists and psychiatrists to help navigate this conundrum. Others wake up one day, realize they are simply "sick and tired of being sick and tired" and they move forward in life without alcohol. For others, it's a single, rock bottom moment—or twenty. There's a further unfortunate group that experiences a lifetime of painful rock bottoms, but never recognizes the problem. The fact that you're reading this book eliminates you from this last group.

Don't worry, shortly, you can take the most accurate, simple "do I have a drinking problem test" ever created. I've found this test 100% accurate and for some, immediately after taking it, they will feel a tremendous weight lift from their shoulders.

But first, let's address why is this question is so hard to answer. For starters, the thinking brain does everything in its power to convince us that our relationship with alcohol is normal, even healthy. Mostly because we think everyone and their dogs drink as much as we do and, thanks to the stigma surrounding addiction, we do our damned best to avoid giving more than a cursory glance at the issue. Another reason is because the current benchmark for what an "alcoholic" or someone with a drinking problem looks like is completely inaccurate. What I have found while doing the Recovery Elevator podcast, after interviewing over 250 people who have decided to move into an AF life, after conducting countless surveys and reading thousands of posts in the Recovery Elevator online community Café RE, is that people who struggle with alcohol don't look anything like what we think an "alcoholic" is supposed to look like. Studies show that 5% of alcoholics fit the stigma of what we think an alcoholic is (homeless, unemployed, drinking from a brown paper bag, etc.). The other 95% live in wonderful homes, have successful careers, are loving spouses, are community leaders, have money in the bank and overall, are kicking ass in life. I've learned that alcoholism does not discriminate. In the online private communities, we have males, females, moms, dads, brothers, sisters, doctors, lawyers, engineers, dentists, and more. This has nothing to do with brainpower, morals or the amount of willpower one possesses. There is no single demographic or stereotype that someone who struggles with alcohol fits in.

When I was acquiring sponsorships for the podcast, I asked over 400 listeners and community members to fill out a demographic survey and here's what I found. The Recovery Elevator community is 55% female and 45% male. 52% are married, with another 24% in a significant relationship. 61% have college degrees, 15% have a master's degree and 12% have a PhD. Their average individual yearly income is 85k. What I found is that the typical "alcoholic" here looks nothing like what someone might think. They are highly professional, educated, high earners, and are in loving relationships. The majority of "alcoholics" not only keep up with the Joneses, they *are* the Joneses. If you were to compare the survey results to national averages, you'd find this group to be well above average. They are high-functioning individuals, and this doesn't surprise me a bit. Some of the most intelligent, successful, loving and caring people I've met have struggled with alcohol.

Another reason it's difficult to self-diagnose the question of 'do I have a drinking problem', or 'am I an alcoholic', is because it's no longer a yes or no answer, but rather where you sit in a vast gray area. The HBO documentary *Risky Drinking* does a good job of explaining this gray area. It places the spectrum of problem drinking into five categories: no risk, low risk, mild, moderate and severe risk. The documentary estimates that only 15% fall into the severe risk category while everyone else (including normal drinkers) sit elsewhere on this spectrum.

Do I have a drinking problem?

People often ask me if I think they have a drinking problem. First off, and this should come as a relief to some, only you can answer this question. I usually have a good idea and have honed in my "drinking problem radar" over the years, but you're the one who has to reach the conclusion. It won't do much good if I say, "Hey, Rick, dude, you've got a level 10 drinking problem on your hands," if Rick isn't on the same page. Rick is the one that ultimately has to make the call.

Listeners often send me long, detailed messages about their drinking history followed by, "Do you think I have a drinking problem, Paul? Sometimes this is even comical, but again, the mind does a damn good job of convincing us we don't have a problem with alcohol.

Here are two examples of emails I have received (with names, dates and locations, etc. changed, of course) where listeners are unsure whether they have a drinking problem or not. What do you think?

Paul,

I've been listening to the podcast for several months and I have really enjoyed the topics and guests. However, I haven't heard a guest who has a similar story to mine and I'm questioning whether I should quit drinking or not. I'm 42 years old, live just outside Chicago, have a good job, a loving family and kids. I started drinking at the age of 14 and it wasn't much of an issue for a couple decades. In my twenties I would go several days or weeks without drinking and not even notice it. However, in my early thirties, after my son was born, the drinking started to escalate. I'm in software sales and a big part of job is dining out with prospective clients. It became difficult to only have a few drinks at these dinners and often times I would arrive early and have two to three drinks before the person I was supposed to meet arrived. I made a complete ass out of myself at a bachelor party in my late thirties when I backed a golf cart into a pond. Sure, everyone thought it was funny, but I was drunk and internally, I wasn't laughing. The past couple years I can only count a handful of nights where I didn't drink. I usually stay up after my wife and kids go to bed and continue to drink. I do my best to keep it to just beer, but occasionally I get into the harder stuff and I pay dearly the next day. My wife has asked me to cut back a couple of times, and I do, for a month or two, but it always seems to pick back up. I don't have any DUIs and have never been fired from work due to drinking. I don't think I've listened to every episode and I was wondering if you've interviewed someone with a similar story. What are your thoughts on my drinking?

—Jason

Outside looking in, yes, Jason needs to ditch the booze and he eventually made this decision. Here's another one from a woman named Jennifer.

Hey Paul,

I had a friend recommend your podcast to me and I listened to probably 5 in a row while working outside yesterday. My sister also has a Standard Poodle, they are the best dogs. Say hello to Ben for me! I was wondering if you could shed some light on my drinking and give me your opinion if I'm an alcoholic or not. I just got out of a relationship with a guy and decided to move back to San Diego to be closer to family and for a fresh start. The guy broke up with me because he said I drink too much, but I don't think I drank that much more than him. I've done and said things while blacked out, but I always apologize, and things are fine. In a previous relationship, I wrecked my boyfriend's car while driving drunk. Although I've been pulled over twice while driving drunk, neither resulted in a DUI so I still have a clean driving record. I'm in my early thirties and I think I drink as much as my friends. Even though I drink wine almost every night, I still go to the gym every day and never drink alone. Over the past couple of years, I've noticed that it's becoming harder to stop drinking once I start. It was 2-3 drinks per night, now it's 3-4. I just successfully did dry January with some friends and I feel great. What's your opinion? I have been battling with depression the past couple years and I feel once the depression lifts, things will be much better. Thanks, Paul.

—Jennifer

The question of "do I have a drinking problem or not," is most likely answered in the first 9 words of this email.

As mentioned earlier, answering the "do I have a drinking problem?" question is difficult because a.) our addiction will eloquently lie to us in our own voice, b.) the stereotype of what an alcoholic looks like isn't correct and c.) thanks to the stigma, we do our best to justify to ourselves and others that we don't have a drinking problem. In addition, I've met several people who identify as someone with a drinking problem yet didn't experience increased tolerance or a physical dependence on alcohol and never experienced a hangover. There's no magic number of how many drinks a person needs to consume to fall into the alcoholic category. In fact, surprisingly, most heavy drinkers aren't alcoholics. A recent study of nearly 140,000 adults by the Centers for Disease Control and Prevention found that nine out of ten heavy drinkers are not dependent on alcohol and many can stop drinking immediately with relatively few side effects. Science still can't yet fully explain why some heavy drinkers become physiologically dependent on alcohol and others don't. Scientists don't know what quantity it takes to cause major brain changes, or if the brains of someone who wishes to quit drinking are different than the brains of a normal drinker to begin with.

Yes, this can be an incredibly tough question to answer, but lucky for you, shortly you will take the most accurate self-assessment test I've encountered. This test is more accurate than the National Council on Alcoholism and Drug Dependence (NCADD) Questionnaire, The John Hopkins University Drinking Scale and the CAGE Questionnaire developed by John Ewing M.D. Believe me, I've taken them all.

Okay, let's get started. There is no need for pen and paper for this test. All you need to do is answer one simple question but before doing so, I want you to take a few deep breaths. The answer to this question may change the course of your life forever. Do your best not to answer this question from the thinking part of the brain but answer from the heart. Are you ready? Question #1.

Have you ever wondered if you have a drinking problem?

Great job! The test is over. That was easy enough right? Phew, you made it! Nice job. Yep, that's it. That's the test, it's that simple. And here are the results, which are also simple. People who don't struggle with alcohol don't ask themselves this question. The simple fact that you're asking this question, answers the question. I've asked hundreds of normal drinkers if they've wondered if they have a drinking problem and the answer is always "No." I remember asking my brother Mark this question and his response was, "Um... no." It's usually this simple.

I'm hesitant to add variations of the same question in hopes of keeping things simple, but what the hell. There are countless ways we can answer the million-dollar question by asking ourselves similar questions. Have you ever tried to cut back on your drinking? Have you entered "do I have a drinking problem?" or anything similar into a search engine? Have a you ever listened to a recovery podcast? Have you done an alcohol challenge such as dry January? Have you ever emailed a recovery podcast host asking if you have a drinking problem? Have you ever told yourself you're going to cut back on your drinking? Have you ever told yourself it's the job, depression, anxiety or life situation and not the alcohol? Have you ever read a book titled *Alcohol is SH!T*, that is housed in the self-help section of the bookstore? Simply asking any variation of these questions essentially answers the question at hand. There's no need to make it more complicated than that.

Again, normal drinkers don't ask these questions, because they don't have a problematic relationship with alcohol.

It took me nearly a decade to answer this question. I remember taking an online alcoholic self-assessment survey in college. The fact I even took the survey answers the question. My college roommates weren't taking online alcohol assessment quizzes. Yes, I had a drinking problem—LONG before I realized. About ten years before I realized. We all know addiction is dangerous, but here is where it gets vicious. Even if I had come across this incredibly simple and in my opinion, the most accurate self-assessment test ever, I'm not too convinced it would have changed much. I still had to go through incredibly painful moments and it nearly cost me my life. I still had to have a failed suicide attempt in August of 2014, before I was ready to quit drinking. This is the power of the most dangerous drug on the planet called alcohol. I feel the most threatening part of the journey, where we are at the most risk of crossing a line that we cannot return from is during the "do I have a drinking problem?" part. Once we fully realize, consciously and unconsciously, that we have been duped by alcohol, the weight immediately starts to lift, and the journey ahead becomes clearer. Don't worry. If you did answer "yes" to this question, life isn't over. A new chapter in your life is about to get started. One filled with joy, optimism, hope, love and compassion for yourself. You will no longer live a life where nearly every aspect is governed by a drug, alcohol. True freedom and liberation are just around the corner. It is my goal in this book to shine the light on the absurdity of alcohol, so the reader doesn't have to experience such intense physical and emotional lows before making the decision to move forward in life without alcohol.

Saddle up

☐ Ask yourself how you're doing? How do you feel? What emotions are you feeling?

☐ Have you ever convinced yourself you don't have a drinking problem? Or justified your drinking? How did this look?

☐ What do you think someone with a drinking problem looks like?

☐ Have you ever put any rules into place in hopes to control or moderate your drinking?

☐ Have you ever wondered if you have a drinking problem? If so, when was the first time that thought arrived? Have you done any internet searches or taken any alcohol self-assessment tests?

☐ What is the result of your simple drinking assessment test?

☐ Ask yourself again if you have a drinking problem. What is your answer? How do you feel?

Chapter 4
The Insanity of Alcohol

*"**You might need to ditch the booze if**...you don't find it the least bit ironic that you hide your empty airplane vodka bottles in your rolled-up vision board in the closet."*

—Leigh, Elizabeth, NJ

As I've already mentioned, recovery, sobriety, quitting drinking and the unfucking yourself from alcohol process is all confusing. There are countless paradoxes, conundrums, and contradictions and we can find ourselves in a pickle at any moment both pre and post getting sober. For example, we drink to relieve the depression, yet alcohol is a depressant. We drink to relieve the relentless anxiety, yet when alcohol leaves the system, anxiety goes through the roof. Alcohol creates and solves problems at the same time. I'll be the first to admit I don't have all the answers. In fact, if at any moment you read the words, "hey guys, I've got it all figured out," please return the book and ask for your money back. There have been countless hand-to-forehead moments on this journey and I've got an inkling there will be plenty more. Keep in mind, we are dealing with a sneaky, slippery, elusive, narcissistic, shit substance called alcohol.

I think anyone who has experienced addiction or recovery personally or witnessed it as a family member, friend, physician etc., will agree this whole process can be perplexing. Usually lightbulb moments allow us a glimpse over a mountain top only to see more mountains, but it's all part of the journey and it's important to cherish each step. I will do my absolute best to share how I successfully quit drinking, how countless others did the same and how you can as well if you decide it's the correct path for you, but first, we need to cover the insanity of alcohol. I'd bet the farm the word insanity was invented to describe addiction to alcohol.

Alcohol blinds us. According to the book *Emotional Intelligence* by Travis Bradberry and Jean Greaves, the average person has 2.3 blind spots. For me, alcohol took this figure out to at least 100. Amy Burrows, a certified Peer Recovery Specialist, says "Alcohol sucks us in and then changes the rules of the game." I read once that alcohol gives us wings to fly, but eventually takes away the sky. Part of the lunacy is a deep, unconscious obsession with alcohol on the physical, mental and spiritual level. We aren't aware of it at the time (hello, blind spot), but we are forging an intense bond with alcohol and for many of us, it becomes our best friend. Once this union with alcohol is formed—and for many this happens unconsciously after the first drink—we become hyperaware of its physical location, how much is on hand and whether the supply will run out. An interviewee on the podcast once said, "If you ask me how much money is in my bank account, I can only give you a rough estimate at best. With beer in my fridge, I know how much, what brand, which shelf and if it's hidden from my wife and kids."

Alcohol is fucking clever. It convincingly tells the consumer, even though alcohol is clearly the culprit, that alcohol isn't the problem. If this is a disease, it's the most ruthless disease of all time. It's a disease that tells you that you don't have the disease. Fuck, that's treacherous. People with scoliosis don't suddenly get a thought that today is good day to run a marathon. People with stage four skin cancer don't stand up suddenly and say, "I need to work on my base tan for the summer." I'm extremely allergic to horses, and although the idea of galloping in the mountains on horseback sounds enticing, my brain hasn't convinced me to do so.

Hollywood often has difficulty portraying the mind games that alcohol can play but *Leaving Las Vegas* with Nicolas Cage gets it right. The countless ways we justify our drinking even when life has presented clear signs that alcohol is doing more harm than good is staggering. We punish ourselves in the gym in order to earn the drinks. We put in long hours at the office, giving ourselves permission to unwind at happy hour with co-workers. We make countless promises to ourselves that are never held. I personally tried to quit drinking every day for the better part of half a decade. Upon waking up, I would promise myself—and oftentimes I verbalized this promise to my Standard Poodle, Ben—that I was done drinking. "Hey Ben, sorry I forgot to feed you last night when I was too drunk and I know it's been a light week for walks, but that's all going to change because I'm done drinking. Today, once this pounding headache dissipates, we are going on a long hike, to your favorite lake. It's going to be incredible. It's such a nice day out." There was no room to misinterpret this internal and external declaration. Even Ben got it. I was done drinking. Forever. Today was the first day of the rest of my new life. So why was it that almost without fail, I found myself drinking later that same day? I can still see Ben's deep brown eyes (I'm tearing up as I write this) staring up at me with unconditional love, saying, "It's okay, dad, I know you'll get this figured out, there will be plenty of time for walks, hikes, runs later. I love you regardless. Just do your best to remember to feed me." Perhaps the unequivocal love a pet shows is the best example of how we need to treat ourselves and others who struggle with addiction.

This declarative morning routine happened at least 200+ times from 2012-2014. The cognitive dissonance is exhausting and demoralizing. We will cover in the next chapter why it's so hard to get a message past the analytical part of the brain to the unconscious mind.

Here is a glimpse of what this insanity looked like for me as my drinking ramped up in my early twenties. I studied abroad in Granada, Spain in the spring semester of 2003 and did what most college students do while studying abroad: party. This Mediterranean country takes the word "nightlife" to a near-offensive level. This love for "la marcha" (party) landed me back in Granada in the summer of 2004 where I organized a pub crawl with my best friend Sean and his two friends, Jared and Jeff. We ran four pub crawls a week, at 10 euros a head and averaged 55 customers a night. This was without a doubt the wildest summer of my life and could be another book in itself. Three weeks before I graduated from Chapman University—great school, by the way, and they did an alumni spotlight on Recovery Elevator in the Spring of 2019—in

November of 2004, even though I had lined up a finance job in southern California, I knew that the future didn't involve me working at an investment banking firm. I was moving back to Spain to either open or buy a bar.

In December of 2005, after moving in with my parents in Edwards, Colorado, working three jobs and saving up nearly 25k in one year, I returned to Granada, Spain where I purchased a bar called Dolce Vita. At the age of 23, I was a co-owner of a bar, living in one of the most beautiful places in the world. Every night was a party till the sun came up. Girls, unlimited friends, VIP tables at clubs, and weekend excursions to the Canary Islands, Amsterdam, and Portugal were the norm, along with tapas every night for dinner. I had MADE IT. Still, within one year my body was giving me clear signals that alcohol was causing more harm than good, but I wasn't ready to listen, and I didn't think alcohol was the problem. In fact, looking back, there were clear signs my drinking wasn't normal even before graduating from college.

By January of 2007, after two years in Spain, I was blacking out 5-7 nights per week and 20-25 drinks per night was the norm. At the end of each shift, around 3 a.m., I would put 3-4 shots of vodka in a to-go cup for the walk home. Regardless of what time I went to bed, my internal alarm clock would wake me up at 5:58 a.m., right before the convenience store across the street opened. Since I was unable to sleep unless enough alcohol was in my system, I would put on slippers and shuffle down to the store and buy one box of wine and two 12-oz. cans of beer for under $2.00. Alcohol is silly cheap in Spain. I even did the textbook move of switching up the convenience store or I would lie to the clerk, telling him that I just got off work, or that I was having an after-hours party at 6:30 a.m. in my apartment. I'm not kidding, I remember saying these things. I would then return to my apartment where I would pour the wine into a glass and start chugging. Between gulps of wine, I would pour the beer into a glass and microwave it so I could drink it faster. With this strange system, I was able to drink the box of wine (1 liter, which is more than a bottle of wine) and two beers in under five minutes. I then would go back to sleep till probably 1 or 3 p.m. This was my sleep routine for the last year owning the bar... and I still was oblivious to alcohol being a problem.

One Sunday, about 18 months into living abroad, I woke up around 4 p.m. with a strange feeling in my stomach and chest. It got so bad that I ran downstairs, jumped into a cab and said, "Take me to the emergency room as fast as you can, I'm having a heart attack." At the hospital, they quickly ruled out the heart attack and I was told to wait in the waiting room. I saw a payphone, dumped a bunch of euros into it and called my mom. I remember telling her, with tears streaming down my face, that "I can't beat this." At the time, I didn't know what "this" was referring to, but looking back, it was alcohol. I was over 5,000 miles from home, completely defeated and completely alone.

When I was seen by a doctor, he told me I had had a panic attack and that anxiety was the reason it felt like my insides were in a blender. He gave me a benzodiazepine (valium) and told me to cut back on my drinking. A panic attack? Anxiety? This was all new to me. Since anxiety is the fucking WORST, I decided to take a timeout from the bar and Spain, and I headed back to the States. Unfortunately, the anxiety would stick around until I fully removed alcohol from my life a decade later.

So I flew back to Colorado, and apart from a few drinks on night 23, I went 30 days without alcohol. I then returned to Spain, fully convinced I didn't have a drinking problem because after all, I just logged 29 days without alcohol. There's no way someone with a drinking problem could do that, right?

Upon returning to Spain, within a matter of weeks I was back to chugging box wine and warm beer at 6:10 a.m. just to sleep. At month 34 I made probably the best decision I could have made. I swallowed my pride and walked away from the bar for good. I don't think I would have survived if I had stayed much longer. Toward the end, I would lock myself in my room and drink hard alcohol for 2-3 days straight without eating. One night, during a blackout, I took 4 Ambien and slept for nearly two days. I'm seriously lucky to be alive. On the plane ride back home, I was experiencing audible hallucinations which lasted for another three weeks. Fortunately, these hallucinations consisted mostly of the

London Symphony Orchestra since I went to bed to The Braveheart Soundtrack nearly every night while in Spain. Unfortunately, hearing things that aren't real is terrifying. The ten-hour flight back to Colorado was brutal—I was sweating, shaking, and hearing things that other passengers weren't. However, despite my pride and ego being crushed, there was serenity in the departure. Taking comfort in the belief that my drinking would stay on the Iberian Peninsula, that it wouldn't cross the Atlantic, I began a new chapter, one I hoped wouldn't involve as much alcohol. That was the plan, at least.

Upon my return to Colorado, I continued to drink, but not nearly to the extremes I did in Spain. Since the anxiety persisted and was now accompanied by its dear friend, depression, I met with a therapist. After getting her up to speed, I remember her tactfully asking me if I thought I had a drinking problem. Despite nearly not returning from Spain alive due to my drinking, my response was a stoic and steadfast, "No." Here's the crazy part. I wasn't lying to her. I couldn't see that alcohol was the problem despite what I had just experienced over the past couple years in Spain. Apparently, I convinced my therapist and we decided not to discuss the drinking and we increased the dosage of my antidepressants (I will cover these meds later). I also convinced myself that alcohol wasn't the problem and I continued to drink for another seven years.

Again, my story is not unique in this regard. The unconscious mind will do everything in its power to mask the true culprit. I've spoken to hundreds of people who have quit drinking and they experienced the same irrationality with alcohol. The same blindfold that I wore. Let's take a look at some examples:

"Janet," my drinking brain voice, would tell me that since I did a great presentation at work, or closed a big opportunity, or just completed a to do list that I sooo deserved a lovely glass of wine. So, I would think, ok, just one with lunch—ok, 2...then maybe head over to a local craft brewery around the corner, they have Wi-Fi....why not finish up any admin work there? So, I would. Two more drinks there. My husband would then call and ask if I wanted anything from the market. Sure, how about some "juice," my chic

code word for Sauvignon Blanc. He will never know I've already had a few...(he always did, as it turns out). Sneaky "Janet."

—Sarah, 46, San Diego, CA

One night I went out to a concert with a sober friend in which I had only a couple beers in front of him but went to the "bathroom" a lot in which I would go to the bar and buy multiple double shots to have before going back to the concert. After he had to take care of me that night, he came over the next morning to tell me he was worried about me and that I might have a problem with alcohol. He gave me some numbers of people that he knew from A.A. that I should call just to talk to. "I DON'T HAVE A PROBLEM WITH DRINKING!" I screamed. I had to scream because I was slowly realizing that all these things weren't normal ways of drinking. In order to shut out these realizations my alcoholic voice had to scream and yell to silence the truth. The truth that I didn't drink normal. The truth that I had a problem with alcohol. The truth that I can't have just one drink. The truth that I'm an alcoholic. The truth was finally surfacing, and I didn't want to hear it. It took another six months after that night for me to finally hit my rock bottom and realize I did have a problem and sober up for good.

—Alicia, 30, Bellingham, WA

At 17 I had my first sip of booze and fell in love. My girlfriends and I would pass the bottle of Blue UV around my family's hot tub each taking pulls. I fell in love with that light, bubbly, giggly feeling as my worries slipped away and my inhibitions lowered. That's the feeling that I tried to chase, that I became addicted to. At 18 I got my first underage drinking ticket, at 19 I got another...three years later it was an operating a vehicle while intoxicated charge (I spent the night in jail because I was so drunk I couldn't give the police the right phone numbers to call my family). Two years after that I woke up in a detox facility after drunkenly walking out of a bar and getting separated from my friends and passing out in an alley (I had to wait until 2 p.m. the following day to blow zeroes and be released). I was then mandated to go to an AODA counselor who after evaluating me said I had a dependence on alcohol. My response was anger and disbelief. How dare he say I have issues with alcohol! I had told him the truth and answered his questions honestly and still couldn't see how I had a problem…Even after all of that I continued to drink…..I would circle between three or four liquor stores in order to keep the façade that I didn't have a drinking problem. I remember once being recognized by a cashier for always coming in and buying booze… I literally lied to her face and said she must be mistaken. Sometimes I'd even buy a birthday or holiday card with the booze so I could tell the cashier it was for somebody else. That's how much I didn't want others to view my drinking as problematic… because I knew that the more often I was confronted by other people's judgements about my drinking that I would have to face it… so I just made up lies and circled from liquor store to liquor store to hide from others, but mostly from myself how bad my problem had become. I was lying to myself and the people closest to me. I didn't really learn that moderation was an option and binge drinking wasn't the only way to drink until about seven or eight years after I'd started to drink… then came a few years of trying to moderate… I'd be successful for two or three events/parties and then slip back into over-indulgence…

—Katie, 28, Madison, WI

It's 3 a.m. and pitch black as I come to. Seconds later I feel the familiar dread and nausea rush like a tidal wave over my body. I've done it again. I got out-of-my-mind drunk again last night. How far back into the evening can I remember?

I remember my first drink of the day, opening a bottle of wine and pouring a cool, crisp, sauvignon blanc when I got home and started prepping dinner. I remember bathing the kids, another glass of wine. Eating dinner, another. Bedtime stories, another. I remember I actually took a glass of wine with me to read bedtime stories, jeez, that's not great. Kids tucked in bed, time to relax, another… husband puts TV on… then I start fading out…I remember fussing about in the kitchen, another, sitting on the deck with another, playing with dog…and then I can't remember anything. I don't remember going to bed. I fucking hate blackouts. My husband never seems to get them, but they are becoming more and more frequent for me now.

I'm so angry with myself. I promised myself I wouldn't drink that much anymore. Actually, I think I said I wasn't going to drink last night at all. How much did I drink? Definitely more than one bottle of wine, I remember opening the second. I wonder how much of the second bottle I drank? Probably most of it judging by how sick I feel right now.

What the fuck is wrong with me? I hate myself. I feel such fierce contempt for myself and that causes another tidal wave of self-hatred, disgust, and remorse. I promise myself no more. Not today. Today I will not drink. I feel mollified by that thought and take my glass of water back to bed. I fall into a semi-doze. I'm still partly awake. I'm looking at my husband in the dark, wondering now if he hates me. I spend the next three hours having similar thoughts and when the alarm finally goes off to start the day, I am unrested, nauseous, with a banging headache, and emotionally raw. But by noon my hangover will have receded and by 4 p.m. I will be looking forward to my first drink…. I think I'll start with beer today, after overdoing it on wine last night. My promises to myself in the mirror in the middle of the night are long forgotten. I will repeat them again at 3 a.m. tomorrow morning.

—Caroline, 40, New Zealand

When I first started drinking, I was 14 years old. It would be weekends with my friends, and we would split a handle of Captain Morgan's rum and take turns chugging it straight out of the handle with a chaser. Over the next few years alcohol didn't play a huge role in my life, and it wasn't until I made some drastic life changes that I started to drink on a regular basis.

I eventually moved to Baltimore, MD in 2007, the day before my 23rd birthday. In Baltimore I quickly fell into the bar scene—it's easy to do when there are reportedly 50+ bars in a 6-block radius. Drinking and being hungover was my new normal. In 2009 I started to question my drinking. I was drinking at least five vodka drinks each day and when realized this I made the decision to switch to wine because I didn't like the taste so would drink less, obviously…. So first it was the standard bottle. Then it moved up to the 1.5 L bottles. After some trial and error, I decided that Baltimore was the problem so in 2010 I decided that the geographical cure was in order, so I took a job on a yacht that sailed from Maine to the Caribbean.

In 2011 I left my job on the boat and moved to upstate New York. I didn't know anyone, so I just kept on drinking. There were times when I was able to put rules into place such as "no drinking before 7 p.m." and "no drinking unless I worked out for at least one hour," but nothing stuck. By 2014 I was drinking at least 1.5 L of wine per day and quite literally blacking out each night. I would wake up with no memory of the night before. I had no clue if I had fed or walked my dog or if I did walk her my anxiety would be so crushing that I couldn't be more than an eyeshot from my apartment. I was a MESS! But that wasn't painful enough, so the drinking continued for a few more years.

By 2017 I was broken. My anxiety was crippling. I was afraid to leave my house some days and I didn't believe that it had anything to do with my drinking. I just accepted it as my "normal." In November of 2017 I started listening to recovery podcasts and I began to see things differently. I paid close attention to the rules people had tried; I had also tried ALL of them. No drinking before 5:00 p.m., no drinking before 7:00 p.m., no drinks during the week, drinks only on Friday and Saturday, drinks only with people, only wine, only vodka, only one beer, only on days that end in "Y." It was maddening.

Eventually I bought a calendar and started putting stars on the days that I didn't drink and frowny faces on the days I did. I thought the visual would help me, but it didn't. It wasn't until I quite literally became fed up with the hangovers—accepted and surrendered to the fact that I have a drinking problem and just sat there feeling it. In June of 2018, I quit drinking and haven't had a drink since.

—Tiffany, Westminster, MD

For many, even after we recognize alcohol is leading us down the wrong path, the absurdity of alcohol continues. We continue to drink despite obvious consequences. In July of 2014, I got a DUI while driving to work. I spent a night in a suicide-proof jail cell wearing nothing but a large padded vest. Despite it being one of the worst nights in my life, I was thankful that I had finally hit my bottom. It couldn't get any worse... or so I thought. Three weeks later, not only was I drinking, I was driving drunk with a broken taillight. Again, as we have already discussed, this is not an issue of intelligence or a lack of will power or morals. We are dealing with a highly addictive, mind-warping drug called alcohol. Here are some examples of how we continue to drink even when the repercussions are clear.

I never really questioned whether I had a drinking problem. I was a blackout drinker from my very first drunk, at the age of 14. It would be years before I would make the decision to stop. Years that included many hangovers, suspensions from high school, a DUI, a public intoxication, wrecked vehicles, a 5-day hospital stay, losing three jobs, waking up to a broken ankle and having no idea how it happened, and possibly losing a teaching career that I worked so hard for and loved so much.

To say that I am powerless over alcohol would be an understatement. What would be the driving force behind stopping at the grocery store at 6:30 a.m., on the way to work, to purchase a bottle of vodka with the sole purpose being to drink it before my students arrived? Insanity is the only explanation.

A 5-day hospital stay in the ICU, which started with my ex-husband having to carry me to the car because I physically could not walk, ended with the doctors telling me that if I did not quit drinking, I would kill myself. I continued to drink for 10 more years and by nothing short of a miracle and the grace of God I am still alive and kicking.

I have had many days of waking up saying "I'm never drinking again," only to have a drink in hand a few hours later. I first stepped foot in the doors of A.A. ten years ago. I had a sponsor and started working the 12

Steps…only to quit by Step 4. I even quit drinking for a few months here and there. I quit, but I was never sober. In all honesty I didn't really care to be.

—Kerri, 48, California

They say that one drink is too many and a thousand is not enough. When I started drinking, one was never enough but three was just about right. The problem was that, over the years, three turned into four, five, six, and so on until I was sometimes drinking three bottles of red wine at a go. Still, I kept going, despite all the pain from hangovers, missed days of work, and just generally feeling like hell every morning. It wasn't until I began having negative physical symptoms lasting for days that I started to even consider that perhaps I should look at my drinking habits. I would occasionally lose feeling on some of the fingers of my left hand. I knew it was alcohol-related because it only happened when I had been hitting the bottle hard. I still kept on drinking for a year, knowing that I was causing potentially permanent damage to my nerves. I remember that when I first told my wife about these symptoms—although not about the amount of alcohol that I was drinking which I always hid from the family—she, of course, immediately told me to go to the doctor. I took her advice—six months later! By this time, the problem had escalated from very occasional to very often. I went to the doctor and when he eventually got around to asking me about how much alcohol I drink, I flat-out lied to him admitting only to 'a few drinks after dinner.' The crazy thing is that I somehow told myself that I had given resolving the problem a good effort despite my lying. I told myself that nothing could be done, so I kept on drinking. I accepted having numb fingers like I did alcohol—it was just now part of daily life. I continued on this path of self-harm for close to another year before I hit bottom from my heavy drinking, and it's a miracle that I have feeling in those fingers today. This is the nature of alcohol—it makes us act in an insane manner where we can easily ignore the obvious evidence of how it is destroying us.

—Tom, 50, Seattle, WA

What's insane about alcoholic drinking is that there is nowhere else in my life where I have failed so many times and still believed I could do something on my own. For most of us, just the fear of failure will keep us from trying anything, let alone failing once or more. But with my drinking, failure every single day to keep it in check never deterred me from trying it again later that night. The insanity is unavoidable because it appears on so many different levels: drinking because you feel you need it to be social, only to prefer drinking alone anyways; avoiding friends and family you love because you love to drink more; beating yourself up every day physically and mentally, only to go back to it again like an abusive relationship. I've always been proud of the independent and stubborn parts of my personality, but in alcoholism they only created more trouble for me. Alcohol was the ultimate abusive boyfriend, the one I insanely crawled back to every single day, forgetting how much it hurt me the night before. It took years for me to realize how bad the relationship had become. And only now that I am free from it can I really comprehend all the insanity I created and withstood for entirely too long.

—Tricia, 37, Dallas, TX

Alcohol is shit. Without-a-doubt, undeniable, pure unmistakable shit and the problem is, most of the time, we can't see it. There are several tiers of this insanity. At first, we don't see the problem. Then we get a glimpse that it might be alcohol and we do our absolute best to convince ourselves and everyone within a 500-mile radius that it's a non-issue. At the top of this bullshit mountain of lies is the idea we can do this alone, as Tricia perfectly stated in the first line of her experience.

It is my goal in this chapter to expose and shine light on how alcohol can lie to us in our own voice—for you to come to recognize this voice as it speaks and begin to see just how fucking ridiculous and ludicrous alcohol can be.

Saddle up

- ☐ Write a time when you made a promise to yourself regarding your drinking that wasn't kept. What did it feel like then?

- ☐ Have you ever 'earned' your drinks? For example, worked out extra hard at the gym so you can drink later?

- ☐ Have you attempted a geographical cure in hopes to curtail your drinking?

- ☐ Do you think you had a drinking problem before you noticed it?

- ☐ Have there been times when you weren't honest with a therapist, doctor or physician about your drinking?

- ☐ What are some blind spots that alcohol has wanted you to avoid?

- ☐ Write down some times when you continued to drink despite knowing the negative that would follow.

- ☐ Can you see traps that alcohol has set? For example, you've had a long day and you drink alcohol because you think it relaxes you. Or you may be feeling depressed and you feel alcohol will give you a lift when in reality it makes you more depressed.

- ☐ Write down a time when you defended or justified your drinking to yourself or others.

- ☐ Have you been able to notice your addiction lying to you in your own voice?

- ☐ Tell yourself nice job—and breathe.

Chapter 5
Why This Can Be So Hard

"You might need to ditch the booze if...you convince your kids to leave wine for Santa."

—Liz, Medford, OR

Quitting drinking can be hard… I'm not going to bullshit you. Many of you have already reached this conclusion. While it has been the most rewarding decision I've ever made, it has also been the most challenging. Funny how that works… One common thread between people I've met at 12 Step meetings, interviewees on the podcast, and the hundreds, if not thousands of conversations I've had with people who have quit drinking is that it's no Sunday stroll. I'd sell more copies if the book was titled *The Easiest Way Ever Discovered to Quit Drinking That Involves Zero Physical and Emotional Challenges and Can Be Done While Walking on the Beach*… or something like that.

We must first eliminate the external toxin alcohol, but then we must go internal. If you go far enough on this path, this is where it will inevitably take you: within. You'll reach a point in sobriety where there are no more forks in the road. The reason why this journey can be so difficult is because removing alcohol is only part of the equation.

We initially think alcohol is the main driver of pain in our lives. It definitely plays a significant role, but it's more nebulous than that. I can guarantee there will be times when you want to hit the "fuck it" button. I said "fuck it" hundreds of times before it stuck. There will be times when you'll want to toss this book into the fire and head straight to the liquor store. You might find yourself saying, "This Paul Churchill guy is full of shit, I've tried everything he mentions, and I still can't put the beast back into the cage." That's okay. It's all part of the process. Just don't permanently quit on me.

Yes, this is a challenge, and some struggle more than others. I've met some that wake up one day and realize it's time to move forward in life without alcohol—for good. This "spontaneous sobriety" is rare, but it does and can happen at any moment. They successfully get the message to the unconscious part of the brain on the first couple tries. For many, like myself, it's a more difficult process getting the memo to the unconscious mind and it takes time. Despite telling myself hundreds of times that I was done drinking, forever, it took much longer to stick.

So why is this? Yes, we have covered how insidious and addictive the drug alcohol is, but why do some seem to "get it" faster than others? Why do some people make a decision to quit drinking and they don't return to the bottle, while for others, including myself, that return was a regular occurrence? Why do some go back to drinking after years of abstinence from alcohol, despite having a good inkling of what will happen if they drink again?

There was something HUGE I missed when I began this journey. This is something I'd estimate 99% of people overlook when they start exploring an AF life. If I were to have first addressed this core problem, it could have transmuted every other issue in my life, including alcohol. No joke. This isn't an exaggeration. Sarah Hepola, in her book *Blackout*, has a line about how she is constantly downgrading addictions, and this rang true for me as well, because I didn't start at the true source of the dysfunction. When we don't address the source of unease, then it's only a matter of time before other addictions start to present themselves.

This "addiction whackamole" is where we might push down alcohol, but the pull to cover up internal discomfort arises in a different part of life. This is a clue that the primary issue has not been addressed. I want to be clear, "downgrading" addictions is still progress, and you are on the right path, but this circuitous route can be exhausting and time consuming. Had I started at the true root of the disfunction, then the alcohol, the nighttime binge eating, the excessive exercise and work, the loneliness, the anxiety, stress, depression, lower back pain, feelings of unworthiness, caffeine, nicotine, antidepressants, ADHD meds, trichotillomania (I used to pull at my eyebrows until there were visible gaps), shame, guilt, inflammation, fatigue, restlessness, feelings of alienation and the despair would have dissolved in time. It's okay. If you're like me and didn't start here either, that's completely fine because life will present you with plenty of opportunities to address these issues the further down this path you go.

I remember the first time that I heard the phrase "drinking isn't the problem… but a symptom." I wanted to slap the guy who said it. Drinking, alcohol isn't the problem? WTF? This guy is on Pluto and has no idea what he's talking about. Are you kidding me? You're telling me that what I just went through in Spain, blacking out nearly every night for three years with death lurking in the background of every binge— and alcohol wasn't the problem? Okay, maybe it was the lack of salt in the Spanish diet. Not the problem? Are you serious…!? Fast forward to a couple years later and gosh dang, that guy was right. Alcohol isn't the problem. It's what we use to make some of life's discomforts more tolerable.

Okay, let me add some clarification to this statement. Alcohol is a major problem when we are physically addicted to the drug. Going "cold turkey," from alcohol is extremely dangerous and I highly recommend seeking medical attention during this process. Alcohol is one of the few drugs (some say the only drug) in the world that you can die from during detoxification. As we learned in previous chapters, alcohol can wreak havoc on the physical body. Yes, in the short term, alcohol is a significant problem. However, after a detox period of 3-21 days, depending on the person, alcohol isn't in the system and we are no longer physically dependent on alcohol. One would think the problem has been solved by removing the toxin alcohol, but it's not quite that simple.

It's easy to think that the departure of alcohol involves fewer rules than Fight Club. Step 1: Stop drinking alcohol. Step 2: Continue to stop drinking alcohol. Nailed it! Peace. End of book… Not so fast. I wish. We can't fault ourselves when we begin the "unfuck ourselves" process, for thinking that simply removing alcohol will create a panacea effect and solve all unrest in life. One of my favorite lines I've heard is "If you want to figure out why you drink, quit drinking and you'll find out pretty quick."

The true source is even sneakier than alcohol and humans have been blind to it for millennia, but we're starting to come around. There have been notable human beings in the past 2,600 years who have seen this dysfunction as the source of all suffering, but most of us don't. In fact, previously I said that 99% of people miss this, but I'm going to modify it to 99.99% of people who can't see the initial road block and I fell into the 99.99% category. It's not the alcohol that causes the insanity described in the previous chapter. The alcohol isn't to blame for the countless failed promises we make ourselves. Alcohol isn't the quandary. It's the telegram. It's a signpost. It's a nudge. It's a pigeon carrying the most important message you'll ever receive.

The problem is thinking, and for most, this is the core addiction.

Saddle up

☐ Have you experienced addiction whackamole? Have addictions shown up in different arenas in your life after removing alcohol?
☐ Do you agree with the phrase, "Drinking isn't the problem, but a symptom?"
☐ Do you think you've been using alcohol to cover up inner pain?

Chapter 6
The Thinking Trap

"You might need to ditch the booze if...you have a glut of birthday cards because it's never suspect to buy a bottle of wine WITH a birthday card."

—Beth, Vancouver, WA

The human brain is the most amazing processing machine on the planet. At this moment in time, it's by far the most powerful computing machine. There are 2,500,000 gigabytes of storage space in your brain. There are roughly 100 billion neurons in the brain (roughly the same number of stars in the Milky Way) with another 1 quadrillion (1 million billion) connections known as synapses that fire up to speeds of 280 MPH. At the time of this writing, the fastest supercomputer in the world doesn't come close to the processing speed of the human brain. In 2014, researchers in Japan tried to match the processing power in one second from one percent of the brain. That doesn't sound like much, and yet it took the fourth fastest supercomputer on the planet (the K Computer) 40 minutes to crunch the calculations for a single second of brain activity. Perhaps the most impressive feature of this three-pound supercomputing machine is its restorative capacities. This neuroplasticity allows the brain to form new neural circuits and fully heal damage that alcohol may have caused. The brain's capability of rewiring itself allows us to write a new narrative and completely depart from the past.

The thinking brain is a powerful tool. But just like any tool, there are many ways to use it. Let's take a hammer for example. You can build your dream home with it or you can go into a museum and destroy everything in sight. For some, the thinking brain can be used to create a wonderful and happy life. For others it can fabricate an internal prison. As the grips of my addiction tightened, I experienced the latter of these two.

The human brain has 60,000-70,000 thoughts per day and most of them are wrong. In fact, we are probably one of the only species to have thoughts about our thoughts, and most of those thoughts are wrong. A single thought, which is comprised of energy at the atomic level, has the capacity to change our lives. What happens if we hitch our wagon to an incorrect thought? What happens when we start to connect a series of thoughts that aren't necessarily true? Dr. Joe Dispenza explains this in his book, *You Are the Placebo*.

If you think a certain way, you begin to create an attitude. An attitude is a cycle of short-term thoughts experienced over and over again. Attitudes are shortened states of being. If you string a series of attitudes together, you create a belief. Beliefs are more elongated states of being and tend to become subconscious. When you add beliefs together, you create a perception. Your perceptions have everything to do with the choices you make, the behaviors you exhibit, the relationships you chose, and the realities you create.

A single thought, regardless of whether it's right or wrong, can determine the outcome of our lives. These thoughts, which turn into attitudes, which turn into states of being, which create beliefs, which eventually settle at the unconscious part of the brain and this becomes who we are—our personality. According to Dispenza, 95% of who you are by age 35 is a set of memorized behaviors, skills, emotional reactions, beliefs, perceptions and attitudes that functions like a computer program at the unconscious level. Our reactions to present moment events are 95% preconditioned.

How we think and how we feel create our entire states of being and nearly all of these thoughts and beliefs are based on past experiences. Therefore, a couple of things happen. We continue to recreate the past. Familiar past experiences will sooner or later become predictable future experiences. This is why it can be so difficult to exit abusive relationships, stick with a new diet, or move forward in life without alcohol. In addition, when we are creating a future based on past experiences, we start each day not in a state of presence but in a whirlwind of past thoughts, and most of them were incorrect from the start.

It's incredibly difficult to get messages to the unconscious part of the brain, especially when we're blind to the hundreds of unconscious programs on autopilot. The conscious 5% is constantly bumping up against the unconscious 95% and this bump turns into a major clash if we are trying to make any significant change in life. It can be nearly impossible to see past the thinking analytical part of the brain if you're not aware of what's happening. Telling the unconscious mind that I'm positively, 100%, without a doubt, never again in my entire life drinking again sounds promising, but only a fraction of that declaration makes it to the unconscious mind. Hundreds of times, I made this a non-negotiable internal announcement and felt confident that a new chapter in life had commenced. Things felt different, then after the passing of a few short hours, the sails began to lose wind and within a matter of time, usually within the same day, I was drinking again. If we are not privy to the power of the unconscious mind, we find ourselves not in the driver's seat of life but being pulled by twine on a wobbly skateboard. The unconscious is clever, and it allows us the belief that we're in control, but we're not. Not even close.

So, what is this thinking/unconscious mind? Who is the unconscious mind? Is it me? Is this who I am? I've got wonderful news for you. No, it's not who you are. Not at all. You are the one that experiences the thinking mind. You are not the voice inside your head, but the one who hears it. Figuring this out on your own is like starting off with a level 10 Sudoku puzzle. The Buddha had to relinquish his life of riches, wander about northern India as a beggar for seven years, then meditate for seven straight days under a bodhi tree before he realized this truth. The ancient Egyptians, on hieroglyphs, display the power of the unconscious mind and how unchecked collective thinking can cause extreme pain and suffering. Another dude named Jesus also recognized this and it became a core of his teachings.

I first learned of this concept on a United flight to Bozeman from Denver, Colorado around one-year AF. A friend of mine recommended *The Untethered Soul* by Michael Singer. At 35,000 feet, soaring above the Rocky Mountains, I remember reading a game-changing sentence:

> *There is nothing more important to true growth than realizing that you are not the voice of the mind—you are the one who hears it.*

I was continuing to read when my body said "Whoa...wait a second, what did I just read?"

> *There is nothing more important to true growth than realizing that you are not the voice of the mind—you are the one who hears it.*

Yep, I confirmed, that's what the book says. You mean I'm not the one constantly calling myself a "fucking idiot" for not being able to quit drinking, but I'm the one who hears it, and not the one who says it? Since my mind was completely blown at that moment, I didn't fully comprehend the idea, but it set the ball rolling. I know this may be confusing, but overall, this is fantastic news when we're looking at addiction and quitting drinking.

There is nothing more important to true growth than realizing that you are not the voice of the mind, but the awareness listening to it. So, if I'm not the voice inside my head, then who is it...? This is the most important action item of this book, and perhaps you're about to make the most important introduction of your life. Are you ready for this? Perhaps put this book down and take some deep breaths first.

Are you ready to start creating space in the mind? To distance yourself from the incessant chatter that was never you in the first place? Are you ready to start being, and stop thinking? Are you ready? I'm pumped for what's about to happen next. You're about to meet a part of you that you initially believed was the full you. Don't worry, no need to put on a blazer or makeup, we are going internal for this one. Are you ready? I think you are.

Here's how you meet this voice. You should be able to get a full view of this person in only a matter of moments. Find a comfortable place to sit and then do this: ask yourself what your next thought is going to be and then wait.... There should be a couple-second pause and then… "why, hello," there it is. That voice isn't you, but your internal roommate. You are not the emotion, the anger, the jealousy, the depression, the anxiety, the addiction, but the one who experiences it.

I don't use the words "game changer" lightly but recognizing this is just that, a total game changer. Since recognizing I wasn't the one calling myself a loser for drinking so much, I was able to start distancing myself from those thoughts. When the voice would say, "Paul, you fucking idiot," (that seemed to be the go-to narrative for a good 15 years), I began to take it less personally. It softened and no longer carried the destructive power it had before. In fact—and this is proof that monumental progress has taken place—around year 3 AF, this internal voice called me a "goofball" for the first time. Simply being aware that this inner voice isn't me has allowed its impact to lighten. I'm now a goofball and not a fucking idiot. Great news! In fact, I've always been a goofball and I've never been a fucking idiot. (Okay, maybe one time when in a drunken state I found myself on the rooftop of my dormitory at Chapman University and thought a pile of bushes would adequately catch me as I jumped off the roof from the second story…fuck, that hurt so bad.)

So why is this voice so hard to recognize? It's because it doesn't want to be discovered. It's a protective personality of sorts, or more commonly referred to as the ego, which is the unconscious mind. I've found we get more work done when we call it the protective personality, but they are both the same thing. Spiritual teacher Eckhart Tolle refers to the ego as a dysfunctional relationship with the present moment. Albert Einstein referred to the ego as an optical illusion of consciousness. Buddhism argues that your idea of who "you" are is an arbitrary mental construction (beliefs based on past experiences) and that you should let go of the idea that "you" or your definition of "who you are" exist at all. It can be argued that the focal point of the 12 Steps of

A.A. is to expose this protective personality. The ego creates an internal prison when we are fully identified with the thinking mind. Most of us (and I know I was) are unaware of a reality without thinking because we have landed upon a sense of self, an identity, based on these thoughts. The ego feels—and this is for the most part true—that part of you would no longer exist if you no longer identified with these thoughts of who you think you are. The less we identify with the protective personality, the easier it becomes to deal with tsunami waves of life when they come. It's possible, to still be comfortable, in extremely uncomfortable life situations. This is because our identity, or "who we are," becomes less contingent on the materialistic or external world. Once our sense of self is no longer derived from stories the mind creates, then even though the waves of life on the surface may be 60-foot swells caused by gale force winds, the sea underneath remains calm.

The protective personality loves routine. No matter how much I wanted to quit drinking, and despite the acute emotional pain, there was comfort living in the hamster wheel of addiction because it was predictable. It was the known. If I were to move forward in life without alcohol, who would I be? What would life be like? Would I be the same person? The protective personality doesn't like exploring this question. It likes a predictable future based off past experiences.

As we grow up, we form a mental construct of who we are based on personal experiences and environmental conditioning. If we choose to no longer identify with this narrative, this sense of self, things can get uncomfortable fast, regardless of how happy or sad we are in life. As the 17th century French Philosopher Descartes said, "I think, therefore I am," and the ego tells us that the only way to survive, to be, is to constantly think. To the protective personality, where you're at right now—this very moment—holds little importance because the ego's survival is based on dwelling in the past or trying to predict the future. The protective personality is constantly concerned with reliving the past because these experiences define who you are and why you act the way you do. The ego relentlessly casts itself into the future to ensure its survival isn't challenged. It does this by incessantly working towards new goals, accumulating external possessions, more things and new experiences. It's the voice inside the head, that says, one day, when I have this job, have a bigger house, significantly more money in the bank and season tickets to the Broncos, I'll be happy. It's responsible for the narrative of "when this happens" or "when the problem goes away," then everything will be okay. If we were able to magically remove all our problems in life, it's only a matter of time before new ones start showing up, and ironically, the ego needs these life dramas to survive.

The trap the ego sets is that all these events occur in the past and future, which pulls attention and focus away from the present moment. We are always seeking a future state of happiness or dwelling on an experience in the past where we were "right" and someone else was "wrong." Even if the protective personality does concern us with the present, it's an incorrect perception, because it says we got here from these past experiences and circumstances, not because we are simply here.

Now that the initial introduction has been made to this protective personality, I want you to start observing the mind as the watcher and not as the one who is thinking. This takes practice. Shit tons of practice. The ego has been at the joystick for decades and it's not going to hand over the reins overnight. The point is to start creating gaps in thinking. At first, these gaps may be a few brief seconds, a couple times a day, but it's important we aim towards forging more space in the mind and body without thought. Observing beauty in nature, such as a sunset or sunrise, is a great way to insert gaps in thinking. Nature has a system built in to naturally create these gaps in thinking for you. Next time you're outside and you see lightning, nature has pulled you into the present moment as you wait to hear thunder. The same occurs directly after you hear thunder overhead as your body awaits the first drops of rain. These true states of "no mind" are nudges from nature to create more gaps in thinking. At first, one to two seconds is all the mind can take without thinking. That's a great start, and we'll continue to build on this.

It's not my point to give the impression that we need to completely annihilate the ego. This isn't possible. There is no thing as permanent ego disillusionment. For many, the goal of doing plant medicine is complete ego annihilation. In fact, when a group of us went to an Ayahuasca retreat in Costa Rica called Rythmia, we had shirts made up that said, "Ego Annihilation Tour, 2019." Complete removal of the ego isn't possible. We need the protective personality; it serves a purpose. The brain is a powerful tool and we need to access the past to make informed decisions for a better future. A paramount goal in this book is to reprioritize the ego. To take it down a couple notches. To question the validity of thoughts that surface from the unconscious mind. To allow thoughts, feelings and emotions to surface without labeling them as bueno or no bueno, and then allowing them to leave on their own. To keep in mind that whatever is coming, is going. No matter how uncomfortable a thought or emotion is, it will pass if we allow it to. You have the ability, and we will deepen into this practice later, to let go of ALL thoughts.

As I mentioned, we do need the protective personality or the ego. It does serve a purpose; however, this part of the human brain is completely under-developed, and a reprioritization of this protective personality is the next phase of human evolution. Our species of humans, "homo sapiens," have been around for less than 300,000 years. If you were to spread your arms out and your wingspan represents the longevity of the human race, our stay would represent the tip of a fingernail. We are a new species that has some serious kinks to work out. To confirm this, all a person has to do is turn on the news or open a history book. The unchecked ego was responsible for over 100 million deaths of our own kind in the 20th century alone. Our species becomes materialist when fully identified with the ego, which never results in long term happiness. For some, this pursuit of materialism can be so strong that it can create a hell on earth, as was the case during the rules of Hitler, Mao Zedong and the Cameroon Regime, to name a few. These are exciting, yet scary times to be a human. 350 years ago, humans were armed with axes and swords while today the human ego has devised ways to end life on the planet with the push of a button. Detaching from the thinking brain is the next stage of human evolution. It has to be. It is this thinking mind that has already compromised the future of humanity.

In his book, *The Power of Now*, Eckhart Tolle explains why the ego, the thinking mind, can be so hard for humans to discover.

> *Because of its phantom nature and elaborate defense mechanisms, the ego is very vulnerable and insecure. The ego sees itself as constantly under threat. Fear seems to have many causes. Fear of loss, fear of failure, fear of being hurt, fear of being alone and so on. But ultimately all fear is the ego's fear of death. To the ego, death is always just around the corner. Fear of death in the ego may present itself in a trivial argument with the need to be right and make the other person wrong. Defending a position in which you have identified is due to the fear of death. If you identify with a mental position, then if you are wrong, your mind-based sense of self is seriously threatened with annihilation. So, you as the ego cannot afford to be wrong. To be wrong is to die.*

As previously stated, the protective ego serves a purpose and is a valuable tool. It's possible to have a healthy or an unhealthy ego.

A healthy ego can look something like this:

- The ability to admit that you're wrong
- Knowing the source of happiness is internal and not external
- Allowing arguments to unfold without having the last word
- Not leaping to defend yourself if you are criticized or insulted
- Recognizing that offensive remarks made towards you don't have much to do with you
- Understanding that everything in life is temporary
- Being able to sit with uncomfortable feelings
- A loving acceptance of yourself and others
- Not taking on other people's problems or struggles
- Being able to establish boundaries with others
- Having the belief that others are doing their best
- Regulating your internal state without an external substance
- Understanding and accepting you don't have all the answers

- Recognizing that the only person you can control is yourself
- Taking responsibility for everything that happens in your life
- Have an understanding that life isn't happening "to you," but "for you."

A healthy ego allows space for joy and happiness. An unhealthy ego, which is usually the result of full identification with mind and thought, can look something like this:

- Allowing a single thought to ruin a morning, day, week or month
- A baseline of stress is present in your life
- The inability to forgive yourself and others
- Defending your ideas, stances and positions at all costs
- Spending a lot of time and energy fighting "what is"
- Attaching happiness to external possessions, places, people and things
- Saying "when this happens" or "when this problem goes away," things will be okay.
- Involving yourself in other people's problems
- Creating unnecessary drama
- Blaming others for unfortunate circumstances in your own life
- Using an external substance, person, or activity to soothe inner turmoil
- Refusal to accept your current life situation
- Constantly waiting for something to happen before life can be tolerable
- An addiction or addictions are present in your life.

In subsequent chapters, we will cover more in depth of how to address the incessant thinking patterns and the reprioritization of the ego. A great way to start is with the breath, and we've already had some "breath breaks" in this book. The ego resides in the past and future, therefore liberation from the thinking mind is in the present and we tap into this with the breath. The grounding power of the breath can be utilized at all hours of the day and not just on the meditation cushion.

Here's an important action item. Insert conscious breathing into different parts of your day, where you place as much attention as possible simply into your own breath. Go ahead and try it now. You may need to place a sticky note on your work desk or set reminders on your smart phone. I have implemented a practice, which I have come to enjoy, taking two to three conscious breaths before exiting the car. While focusing on the breath, I look up and wait till I'm aware of the clouds moving before exiting the vehicle. Nowadays, just like the weather, my body can allow emotions to pass while taking these deep belly breaths. Sounds basic, but it's had a profound effect on my life.

After attending hundreds of 12 Step meetings, interviewing over two hundred and fifty people for the Recovery Elevator podcast, and tracking my own personal experiences, I feel it's safe to say that those who struggle with addiction have overwhelmingly identified with thought. We are living in our heads and gaps of 'no thought' are rare or don't happen at all. After becoming aware of this voice inside my head that was never me in the first place, I quickly realized it never shut up. That it was a nonstop ruminating machine that, at first, I had little control over. I had become so attached with the thoughts of the mind, I was constantly living in the past and future, and there was little to no room for the joy which resides in the present moment.

At most 12 Step meetings this tendency can be observed within a handful of shares. Often the chair of a meeting will start off with a topic. Then the next person will say "great topic," and then proceed to quickly deviate from the subject and talk about their own inner struggles which have nothing to do with the prompt. At some meetings this can continue for a full sixty minutes.

What happens when we cease to incessantly think? When we begin to depart from the thinking mind, we tap into a vast realm of intelligence beyond thought and that cannot be sourced within the thinking mind. Einstein said that the majority of his scientific breakthroughs occurred at a moment when there was no thought, no mind. Most thought leaders, scientists, artists, authors, musicians, inventors, engineers, and more admit that their most profound lightbulb moments or periods of creation came when they weren't thinking. When we are in a state of no-mind, or no-thought, creativity arises. The most creative individuals on the planet—Shakespeare, Mozart, Van Gogh—demonstrate the power of this creative intelligence that we can all tap into once we quiet the mind. Looking back, I recognize that I can't take credit for any of the seemingly good ideas I've had. The idea for the Recovery Elevator podcast, a project to keep me sober, came to me in a state of no-mind. I was standing, or let's go with hiding, behind a tree before entering an A.A. meeting in the fall of 2014. My mind was busy thinking of excuses of why I couldn't attend the meeting. I didn't want anyone to see me, I had work to do, I was too busy, I had 50+ days of sobriety under my belt so, "I got this," (the three most dangerous words someone with a drinking problem can say). My addiction had successfully convinced me that a 5:30 p.m. meeting wasn't necessary, that I was cured for life. Before heading back to my vehicle, something came to me which wasn't in thought format. It came at the gut level. At that moment, I knew I was going drink again if I didn't do something differently. A couple of seconds later, the idea of a podcast, as a tool to hold myself accountable showed up in the solar plexus region of my body. A podcast? Fuck? Really? Me coming out to the world about my goal of quitting drinking in audio format for anyone to hear? No way, not a chance. The idea terrified me, but I knew it had to happen. Without that sliver of no-thought, the podcast doesn't happen. This book doesn't happen. My sobriety probably wouldn't have lasted much longer than 50 days. The inner peace I experience today, that continues to grow within, wouldn't be part of my life without that brief gap in thinking. That's how powerful a single gap in thinking can be.

There's a reason this chapter is placed well before the "how to" segment of this book. Unchecked thinking, full identification with the protective personality, is perhaps the biggest driver in our addiction. We are unable to think ourselves out of addiction because thinking is a primary driver of an addiction. Take a moment and analyze whether you have been able to successfully think yourself into sobriety or moderate drinking. If this were the case, you wouldn't be reading this book. I've asked over 250 interviewees if they have been able to successfully think themselves out of this pickle and I'm still waiting on the first "yes" response. I ask interviewees if they have ever put rules into place with their drinking—no drinks before 5 p.m., never drink alone, switching from spirits to beer, etc. The second part of the question is whether any of these self-invented rules worked. Some clear trends have emerged. All 250 podcast guests have used the thinking mind to create and implement new rules in hopes of controlling their drinking and not one guest has reported a success story over the long run. I'm a firm believer that we can't think ourselves into a better relationship with alcohol. When we do have those breakthrough moments during this journey—saying to ourselves, "I need to tell someone about my drinking," or "Fuck—I can't do this alone, I need to start to start a podcast to create accountability,"—these bits of genuine truth arrive when there are gaps in thinking. This wisdom that arrives in a state of no mind is so powerful that only a fraction of no-thought is sufficient.

Saddle up

- ☐ Ask yourself what your next thought will be. Once that thought comes, recognize this voice as the protective personality or ego. Repeat this process several times. Say hello to the inner roommate.

- ☐ What role do you think the protective personality, or the ego has played in your life?

- ☐ Have you told yourself that when you accomplished something, or made more money, then you would be happy? Did that prove to be true for more than a short period of time?

- ☐ Are there times in the day when you experience "no-mind" or have gaps in thinking?

- ☐ Based on the list above, would you say you have a healthy or unhealthy ego?

- ☐ For a period of ten seconds, give intense attention to the present moment. Were you able to make it the full ten seconds? When a thought did arrive, was it from the past or about the future? Repeat this process several times and tally which thoughts are from the past and how many are about the future.

- ☐ Insert conscious breaths throughout the day. Perhaps after you send an email or text, before you take a drink of water, or before you dry off with a towel after a shower. Place sticky notes or create phone reminders for these breaths so they can become second nature.

- ☐ Honestly, have you been able to think yourself out of a drinking problem? Have any of the rules or moderation methods worked?

Chapter 7
The Invitation and Why It's So Hard to See It

"You might need to ditch the booze if...... you try to take your mascara off with nail polish remover."

—Rose, Dijon, FR

A paramount goal of mine in this book is for you to change your relationship with alcohol, but in a way you probably didn't imagine. The goal is for readers to eventually reach a point where they say "thank you" to alcohol. I'm sorry to add another layer of complexity to this book, but that's where this path leads us if we go far enough. Eventually, we'll know that we're on the right path when we hold a tremendous amount of appreciation for alcohol. For the invaluable lessons that alcohol has shown us along the way. In time, you'll arrive at a point in this journey where tears of gratitude will stream down your face towards alcohol. If this hasn't happened yet, KEEP GOING. Eventually, you'll recognize that alcohol isn't the villain, it's the reason you have a better life today. As I mention earlier in this book, alcohol is a spirit, which can give us profound gifts if we're able to recognize it. This spirit can provide the road map to a life filled with inner peace, joy, love, compassion and happiness, if we are ready to listen. It has the ability to open up the heart and create space for joy, happiness and inner peace. Alcohol invites us to wake up from hibernation and get into the driver's seat of life again.

An addiction isn't something to overcome. It's not a foe. I didn't beat or overcome my addiction. Thanks to alcohol exposing areas of my life that needed to change, I was able to work with the addiction and change the course of my life.

We don't beat addictions—we listen to them and make the necessary changes. We use their force to shine light on the correct path. We work with the addiction to reveal what we were using alcohol to cover up in the first place, but to do this, we must walk towards the addiction and not away from it. Once we do this, eventually we'll have an "aha" moment and say, "Oh shit, alcohol isn't the problem!" It's the invitation to a much better life.

I was at an A.A. meeting once and there were two newcomers in the room. An old timer said to them, "Well guys, I'm sorry it's come to this…" It was followed by a few chuckles and silence. "Whoa, what a demoralizing thing to say to a newcomer," I said to myself. This guy missed the purpose of an addiction. What a grim and completely inaccurate thing to say to a newcomer. The guy speaking (one who makes sure you know how much sobriety time he has every time he speaks), has missed the invitation, or the primary function of addiction, which is to reveal what parts of us need the most healing. I would say most people recovering from addictions miss this. Some view this as a life sentence—a life of attending meetings, that life has "come to this," that the good days are behind us. I've got good news. None of this is true. Addiction is the invitation. In fact, if you're struggling with an addiction, congratulations. You got the invite for a wonderful life depending on how you RSVP… but the fact that you're reading this book tells me how you'll respond.

Some of you might be saying, "Addiction? The invite to a better life? Are you sure about this, Paul?" Well, yes. It feels like things got a little off track. The path you currently find yourself on may have been internally labeled as incorrect, but it's the same path that will lead to you a life filled with bliss and inner peace. This can get tricky when the thinking mind intervenes and tells you that you cannot get there from here. That external things need to happen first before you can start. Perhaps you need to get on a different path first, but to get on a different path, we still must start from here, the path we currently find ourselves on. We had to go down this path to receive the invitation, an invitation that we should start exploring.

Let me tell you a quick story. A guy was shopping at a mall near the coast of southern California. Before leaving, he saw a gorgeous car on display and saw that if he dropped a business card in a gigantic fishbowl, he had the chance to win it. Upon exiting the mall, he dropped his business card into the raffle bowl and didn't think much more of it. Less than a week later, he gets a phone call and he wins the car. Hooray! Two days later, he gets T-boned at an intersection, breaks both legs and an arm and is in rough shape. What's worse, he didn't have insurance on the new car, so it's gone. His friends visiting him said, "Man, that's tough luck, buddy. We're so sorry to hear about this." After two weeks in the hospital, just one day before he is supposed to leave the hospital, he learns of a landslide that took his house out to sea in the middle of the night, never to be seen again. His friends showed up the next day and said, "Whoa, you would have been swept out to sea with your house had you not been in the hospital. You're the luckiest guy on the planet!"

You've never been on the wrong path in life. To be fair, everyone gets nudges and invites in life, including people who don't experience addiction. But for us, these invitations are announced in megaphones inches from our heads – so we should probably listen.

We, this group of incredibly lucky individuals, receive thousands of invitations. So many of them that we currently find ourselves reading this book. At first, these invitations to depart from alcohol may have been disguised as "one-offs:" a bad hangover, or we make an ass out of ourselves at a BBQ, or else they don't show up with enough frequency for us to connect the dots, but over time they show up once a month, once a week, every day, in every aspect of our lives until we can no longer ignore the messenger.

This invitation is alcohol. But what exactly is this invitation? It's an invite to wake up and go within. We reach a point where we can no longer turn our back on an addiction, that we must turn around and look it square in the eyes, and say, "alright, alright, I'm ready to listen. Let's have a chat." We realize negotiations with alcohol are no longer paying off. A day comes when we find ourselves completely exhausted from paddling upstream. When we recognize that little to no progress has been made in fighting the addiction. When we wake up completely exhausted, and sick and tired of being sick and tired, we are ready to RSVP to the invitation at hand and start making the most important change in life. Ditching the booze.

At first, many of us, including myself, say "no fucking thank you," when this proposal presents itself. I declined the invite to an AF life for nearly a decade. But after enough emotional pain, after the bullshit caused by alcohol starts to noticeably pile up, we lift our gaze, stare right into the addiction with a non-judgmental gaze and we experience a colossal "OH FUCK" moment. We begin to recognize the addiction as an opportunity for a better life and not as an anchor that's tied to the ankle. This is a powerful moment in the journey because it's most likely the first time the mind (both conscious and subconscious), body, heart and soul are all on the same page, resulting in a 5-tiered collaborative healing effort. Before, it was all thinking, all protective personality. Now, the strategy has shifted and you're no longer solely relying on the unreliable thinking that got you into this pickle in the first place. Reinforcements have arrived and you're happy to have the help. When the mind (conscious and subconscious) and body start working in tandem, it creates a channel for the heart and soul to communicate. This can be scary and uncomfortable at first because it's a new approach. Once the mind and body start connecting, there may be some awkward moments. Toes will be stepped on as you learn how to walk in tandem. You'll both talk at the same time. At first, they will go in different directions. The body loves Third Eye Blind while the mind loves Alanis Morissette but shortly, you'll be peacefully cruising around with one hand in your pocket and the other one giving a peace sign. The moment we connect the body and mind is when we can start letting things go. The most important function of the mind in the short-term of this journey is to locate the body. Once this happens, you'll find that a substantial amount of sobriety fuel isn't derived from accumulating anything, but from letting things go. When the gap between the mind and body have been bridged, the most important connection has now been made resulting in serene internal unity. As you begin to let things go, something else will arrive. It's warmth, it's light, it's love, and usually shows up in the heart region. This is the best feeling in the world.

This is not a mind trick or even simply looking at it from a different angle? You are too smart for that. Hell, even I'd be able to see through that. If we stick with this long enough, it will become clear that alcohol/addiction were the messengers saying "hey, body, mind, heart, soul, team pow-wow. Change is on the horizon in the very near future and we're going to work together in this effort. Sound good? Ready, break!" The addiction was responsible for launching us forward into a happy life and we'll realize it was the best thing that ever happened, not to us, but *for* us. This brings us to an important action item. Promise yourself that you'll stick with this long enough until you reach this realization.

Some of the most profound and revered thought leaders of all time have struggled with addiction. These people accepted the invitation to connect the body, mind, heart and soul and make lasting positive change in their lives.

Addictions are no more than signposts in life, and this might be one of the most important lines in this book.

Addictions are no more than signposts in life.

Many of us almost miss this invitation. I know I almost did. I almost labeled the entirety of my addiction as bad, as unfortunate, as why-me. I'm not gonna bullshit ya, I went through some tough years. After graduation from college at Chapman University, I moved home with my parents for a year where I saved up $28,000 and then moved to Spain and bought a bar. Three years later, after the biggest ass kicking of my life, I did the ultimate Charlie Brown walk of shame back home to my parents' basement. It was fucking miserable, and I wasn't done. I had to push the boundaries of emotional and physical hell for another seven years before accepting the invitation to move into an AF life. I earned this invitation. 758,879 times. You've earned the invitations. This pain and suffering required to initiate positive change is what philosopher Alan Watts calls "The Backwards Law." Pain and suffering are required to spark the most profound positive change we can make in life and most likely, that beautiful bullshit is behind you. It is often said; one must go through the darkest night in order to get to the infinite light. Extreme challenges in life—and addiction lands near the top of this list—are biologically useful. It's nature's way of inciting positive change. As Freud once said, "One day in retrospect, the years of struggle will strike you as the most beautiful."

In early 2014, I went to an A.A. speaker meeting, where someone shared their story. This younger gal started off by saying "Why me?" I said to myself, "Preach on sister, this fucking sucks." Then she said something that blindsided me. She said, "Why me, why am I the lucky one who gets to stand up here today sober while so many others are succumbing to this disease. Why do I get to share about my incredible life while others continue to struggle with addiction?" As I heard this, my gaze went from the carpet up to the girl speaking. Deep down, I knew she was right.

I heard somewhere that the odds of winning the lotto are 1 in 127 million. I've also heard that the odds of you being you, in this universe, on this planet, reading this book right now are 1 in 400 trillion. I have no clue how people with bigger brains than mine calculated that, but let's roll with it. Not only have you already won the biggest lotto of all-time by being on this planet, you're part of the elite few who get the invitation to "WAKE UP" and step into the greatest dance of all FUCKIN time. You're not a fly, a gnat, a caterpillar or a dog. You're the most intelligent, powerful being on the planet and an AF life is the most precious thing ever.

Sure, alcohol is shit, but it's also the invitation. I love the title of this book, but it could also be argued it's a complete bait and switch, and I'm okay with that. :) Alcohol being the solution and not the problem was the focal point of my talk at the Recovery Elevator retreat that took place in Nashville in February of 2019. I almost scrapped the speech the day before the event because it's a tough concept to put into words. Many people in the room weren't quite at the "I LOVE my addiction" part of their journey yet. At first, there were a lot of blank stares in the audience, but as I continued, for some, it started to sink in. The ultimate RSVP to the invitation of addiction is to awaken, which I experienced at three and a half years from my last drink (and more on this later), but there are several other levels of responses. For example, the fact you're reading this book is a response to the invitation. Or the moment when through sobriety, you are able to see clearly that it's time to leave a toxic work environment, is also an RSVP to the invitation.

Before we close out this chapter, I want you to ask yourself if you've responded to the invitation. At what level? Have both the body and mind responded? While taking a couple conscious belly breaths, ask yourself this question. Do your best to shut off the thinking mind and see if an answer arises. Where does this response come from? The mind? The gut? The solar plexus? The heart?

Again, this isn't a mind trick. Deep down inside, at the heart, soul and source level, your body knows the addiction to alcohol is giving you cues and signals to what changes in life need to be made. The body recognized these invitations for positive change long before the mind did. Once the mind gets the memo and starts working in conjunction with the body…watch out. The ball starts rolling fast.

Saddle up

☐ Do you agree an addiction is here to tell us something? What messages do you think alcohol has been trying to tell you?

☐ Have you ignored past invitations? Write some down.

☐ Are invitations arriving with more frequency and amplitude? Write these down too. Keep a running list.

☐ Promise yourself you'll stick with this long enough until you recognize the addiction was working in your favor all along.

☐ How will you RSVP to the invitation and what's the plan?

Chapter 8
Saying Goodbye

*"**You might need to ditch the booze if**...you use white wine as a mixer for your vodka."*

—Tricia, Dallas, TX

Alcohol became my best friend. We did a lot of fun shit together. Alcohol was with me when I asked Lindsey Brents to prom my senior year as well as when she dumped me two weeks later. It made uncomfortable situations (basically the entirety of ages 13-22) manageable. Alcohol gave me the ultimate pep talk and said, "Paul, me and you can do anything in life." In the beginning, the spirit alcohol temporarily connected the heart and soul creating a sense of wholeness. I envisioned alcohol and I having a long and harmonious relationship lasting well into the final chapter and perhaps final moments of life.

Alcohol worked like a dream for quite some time. From ages 14-22 I drank alcohol with relatively minimal consequences. It allowed me to amplify the level of enjoyment in life while covering up the loneliness from childhood. The problem is that past traumas and emotions don't go away unless they are felt and processed. Alcohol allowed me to push that "noise" into more covert recesses in my body, but eventually they all filled up. I reached a moment where my best friend alcohol turned its back on me, and the relationship became one-sided where alcohol was no longer giving. It was the ultimate betrayal. We each eventually arrive at a crossroads when at the conscious and unconscious level, we know it's time to say goodbye to alcohol.

I'm not going to bullshit you. It feels like we find ourselves in the middle of a 55-car pileup at this moment in the journey. It sucks. When alcohol turns on us, it can feel like a stab in the back, or 50, and it will probably be the most profound breakup we go through in life. Saying goodbye to alcohol was harder than any breakup with a girlfriend, a death of a family member, or when the band I was in my junior year of college broke up.

In this chapter I'd like us to formally break up with alcohol. Like some ex-significant others who don't quite get the message at first, this may take some time, but I'd like for us to say goodbye formally, in a 'Dear John' letter of sorts. Take some time and think about all the memories and experiences you had with alcohol. What was your first drink like? Don't ignore all the great times you two had together. When did alcohol start to turn on you and it no longer delivered what it had always promised? What are some of the worst memories from alcohol? I recommend personifying this spirit and giving alcohol a name. Mine is Gary. He was cool at first, but now he's a total ass. This is an important step and I recommend taking a couple of hours on this exercise. Perhaps go to an old drinking nook in the house and start writing. Let the body do most of the writing.

Below I've included a powerful 'Dear John' letter written by a gal named Michelle. She read this letter at a Recovery Elevator retreat that took place in Bozeman, Montana in 2017. In addition to saying goodbye to alcohol in this powerful letter, she read it in front of a group of people. Way to blast through that comfort zone, Michelle! A LOT of healing took place for everyone and there weren't many dry eyes in the audience. And again, of course all names and details have been modified.

Dear Alcohol,

We met when I was 15. Do you remember? It was at Amber and Tom's house. Do you remember how fun that night was? We mixed together the entire liquor cabinet—from tequila to Bailey's—and added a splash of orange juice for good measure. I painted Jeff's toenails and we sang "I Just Want to Fly" along with the video on MTV. Remember how free we felt?

We met again when I was 16 and was living in Spain as an exchange student. We became close that year. You introduced me to cigarettes, tight clothes and beautiful Spanish men. Men I would make out with in bars, in bathroom stalls. You made me feel confident and flirtatious, beautiful and fun.

In college, I used a fake ID and made sure you were always by my side. More times than I can count, I somehow managed to ingest you while doing a handstand over a keg. Through it all, I got straight As and no one was the wiser that I was slowly developing a problem. Not even me. Though, looking back, I suspect you knew exactly the path we were taking. You sneaky devil.

In London, after college, we drank. Oh my, did we drink. We drank and we sang at the local pub. And we looked at those poor English drunks and thought "How sad, but how lucky I am that that will never be me." We slept with Cooper from Canada that last night, something I never would have done without you, alcohol, pushing me to do it.

After Europe, you held my hand as I moved to NYC, where more drinking and smoking ensued. Living the life! We dated Aaron there and smoked cigarettes with him in bed until 4:00 a.m. Empty wine bottles everywhere. The city teeming all around us, awake at all hours, just like we were. In New York, you taught me to like wine and liquor. You stood by and watched me as I watched Tim, my co-worker from the office, as he seemed to drink more and more at company happy hours. Tim was so supremely uncomfortable in his own skin until he was six shots deep. After those shots, he would light up and relax, seemingly brimming with confidence, only to return to work the next morning, eyes downcast, his light out once again. While I was also learning to drink a bottle of wine a night, I still looked at him and thought, "Poor Tim. Thank God that will never be me."

Next you moved with me to the West Coast. I was heartbroken following a breakup in NYC, but my first night in Seattle I met Spencer over several drinks and when I hooked up with him, I didn't feel so lonely. At least for a few hours. Then we met and fell head over heels for Brady. Brady and I dated for years. We'd throw dinner parties for our friends. I loved dinner parties, where no one was keeping track of how many of those empty wine bottles could be credited to me. Remember those vacations we took with his parents? Where I spent most of the time anxious there wouldn't be enough alcohol to go around? Anxious they were tracking how much I drank. The time his mom caught me drinking champagne directly from the bottle at Christmas when I thought no one was looking. How she never said anything but how she never looked at me the same way again. When Brady and I eventually broke up, you were there like my knight in shining fucking armor. Like a devoted sister, ready to be at my side through the tears and heartbreak. For nearly three years after that breakup, you helped me fill my time with happy hours, wine at home, wine with friends, wine in the rain, wine in the sleet, wine in the sun, wine because it's windy, wine by the fire, wine on the deck, wine alone, wine with mom, wine with [insert any possible scenario here]. You get it.

When going on trips with friends (normal drinkers) I began to always bring my own supply of wine, stowed secretly in my suitcase as I maintained a buzz for the entire trip. Only you and I knew I was having any more than the others, that's how good I was at pretending. At keeping your secret. There are the times when I let you have your way with me altogether: the night of my house warming party, that I'd so carefully prepared for and ended up wasted and sleeping with one of my best friends. I never would have done that if you hadn't been coursing through my system. When I went to Colorado, determined not to drink during the trip, and ended up so drunk at a dinner party I threw up and woke up at 11:00 a.m. the next day, still drunk. The time I listened to the Recovery Elevator podcast for four hours straight on a road trip, only to pull over to a rest area for lunch and pour myself a mug of wine to go along with it. The night in San Francisco when Kirk and I went out for a casual dinner and eight drinks later, found myself wasted yet again. Fuzzy memories of bad sex. Waking up to the worst shame and sadness one can imagine.

For years I leaned on you for support. I thought you were my best friend. Over time, the hungover days at work began to out-number the clear-headed ones. I began to dread the drive to work in the morning, crossing the bridge, sun in my eyes, head slamming, stomach roiling. I used to turn to you to help calm anxiety, but at some point, I started to feel abandoned by you as I woke up at 3:00 a.m. every night, full of panic and remorse. All those times I tried to moderate and completely bombed, breaking every single one of my rules.

The number of times you have betrayed me is impossible to remember and impossible to count. I have lost YEARS of my life to you. People talk about rock bottom and I've found every bottom has a trap door to take you even lower. I have been incredibly fortunate to never have had a DUI, not to have lost my job, to have had no major health ramifications and to still have all of my friends and family by my side. But you have done more than enough damage over the years. My lows may not seem as low as other people's, but they were fucking low enough to scare the shit out of me. And more importantly, I can't imagine going any lower.

So, you know what, my "friend" alcohol? I can't do it anymore. I just can't do it anymore. I am exhausted and I AM DONE. You see, I've been thinking about us a lot. I've come to realize that I have this one life to live. One chance at this. And it's because of you that I'm not doing it right. I AM MISSING OUT ON MY LIFE. I see now that while it's terrifying and sad, I can't have you anymore. Because I am onto you; I know your ways now. I've been doing a ton of research lately. I know you will be back, sometimes as a whisper, and sometimes as a roar. You will tell me that we can be together again. That it will be different the next time. That things weren't as bad as I remember. But God help me, I will do EVERYTHING I can to remember the bad decisions, the foggy memories, the hangovers, the feelings of shame and self-loathing. The feeling of feeling entirely EMPTY because of you. Because you know, this week I told people about you. That's right, they know about you too now. I told Kristin, Megan, Andrea, Claire and my mom. I told them about how dysfunctional our relationship has become, and that I can't trust you anymore.

Telling them about this secret was possibly the hardest thing I've ever done. But you know what, it was raw, and it was real. I finally felt something again, after all these years. When I was drinking, I didn't feel one damn thing.

Paul from the Recovery Elevator podcast has a name for his alcoholic voice. He calls him Gary. I've decided to call you Crazy Asshat Psychopants. I could have gone with something like Sally, but Crazy Asshat Psychopants just has a certain ring to it, wouldn't you agree?

So here we are. I am sad for us. It seemed we had a good thing going for a little while there. But let's be real, it was never really good. And it's time to say goodbye. I can't have the life I want if you are in it. Let me repeat that: I can't have the life I want if you are in it, SO YOU ARE NOT WELCOME HERE ANYMORE.

Goodbye, Crazy Asshat Psychopants, goodbye!

Wow. Great job, Michelle.

After you write your 'Dear John' letter, I want you to stand in front of a mirror and read it out loud. Take a deep breath before beginning. Listen to the voice talking. While reading, take a couple breaks and look yourself in the eyes. Who do you see? Do you recognize this person? It's okay if you don't. We will be connecting parts of you that have been disconnected for years, perhaps decades. When you're finished reading the letter, ask yourself if you would like to read it again. Maybe the next day, or maybe every night for a week. This may be painful, but it needs to be done. If you really want to get after it, read the letter to someone. Perhaps start with a pet and then invite a family member or best friend to listen. It's okay to be sad. Don't fight back the tears, the feelings of shame, remorse, hostility or grief. Let all emotions and feelings come to the surface and feel them. After this exercise, you may feel like a part of you is missing. This is a good thing. You may feel rejected, depressed and lonely for a short time after this exercise. That's okay. Allow it to happen. It's all part of the journey into an AF life.

Saddle up

- ☐ Did you consider alcohol to be a friend? Perhaps your best friend?
- ☐ Did alcohol start to turn its back on you, creating more bad memories than good ones?
- ☐ What did it feel like when alcohol no longer had the desired effect?
- ☐ Write a formal goodbye letter to alcohol. Be sure to give your friend alcohol a name. Include when you first met, how you two got to know each other, some of your best memories together, when you two started experiencing conflict, and be clear why it's time to go your separate ways.
- ☐ Read the goodbye letter out loud while standing in front a mirror. Take several breaks to check-in with yourself.
- ☐ Read the letter to a close friend or family member.

Chapter 9
Laying the Foundation

"You might need to ditch the booze if...you work out HARD for 1.5ish hours and burn approx. 650 calories...so you can have your bottle of wine that night. And you do that almost every day."

—Melissa, Brookfield, IL

Before diving into specific strategies and techniques that will propel us forward in an AF life, there are several core concepts that I'd like to cover in this chapter first. Beginning this journey without a basic understanding of the fundamentals would be like going down a double black diamond on the first day of skiing. I'm sure it's been done, and it can probably be seen on YouTube, but I imagine the outcome isn't pretty. I encourage you to revisit these foundational pillars with frequency throughout your journey because you'll find that some have new meanings when you're at different points in your journey. You're a different person at 30 days alcohol free than you are at day 1. Reading this chapter again after new neural circuits have been built will shine light on an idea from a different angle. Some of these are well known concepts that the whole of the recovery community will agree upon and some are not. Some of these approaches are not mainstream but are paramount. These concepts will be the roots of your recovery and the better your grasp of them, the sturdier the foundation will be.

Awareness

I once heard you could combine the 100 most potent medicines from the west with the 100 most potent medicines from the east and you still wouldn't have the power of Awareness. Awareness will be your number one ally throughout this journey, and I want you to be aware of your thinking as much as you can. As I mentioned before, if we get the thinking under control and depart from full identification with the thinking mind, then this has the power to transmute the bulk of suffering we experience in life, including addiction. Now, hitting the 'off' button on the thinking mind is a TALL order and takes loads of practice, so right now, all I want you to do is start building awareness of your thoughts. Without judgment and attachment, become aware of thoughts as they enter. Do your absolute best not to label them as good or bad; just let them be. We want to start distancing ourselves from those 60,000-70,000 thoughts per day that mostly contain energetic bonds with the past. Imagine you're flying in an airplane at 35,000 feet and your thoughts are the cars, farm fields, trains, lakes and mountains below. Observe them, but don't jump out of the airplane and attach yourself to a specific one. If you see something out the airplane window you don't like, don't ignore it or turn your gaze. Simply observe it, and let it be.

Through this awareness of thought, with non-attachment, as we begin to identify less and less with the thinking mind, a space, a sense of calm, begins to emerge in the body and mind. Awareness is a muscle and it will take time to strengthen. Don't get frustrated if this doesn't happen in your first seven days away from alcohol, it takes time and practice. In addition, it's damn near impossible to build this awareness while doing multiple things at once so please stop multitasking. In fact, the only multitasking I want you to do while reading this book and in life, is to be aware of your thinking while doing a single task. In addition to being aware of thoughts, observe the body's reactions when certain thoughts emerge. Again, don't label these reactions as comfortable, uncomfortable, blissful or painful—just observe.

When you experience a craving, or find yourself in a difficult life situation, become aware of a specific location in the body where the discomfort lives. At this moment, all we need to do is say, "Why, hello there, uncomfortable knot the size of an Easter egg in my solar plexus." These energetic vortexes in the body are the body's stored reactions to the mind. If gaps or space are created around these energetic patterns, which is done by not adding more thoughts (energy) to them, they will begin to dissipate and transmute themselves on their own, as in, you don't have to think yourself out of uncomfortable emotions.

On this AF journey, you may have found things don't necessarily happen in a practical order. As awareness builds around thought, and we identify less with roles, identities, and personas, we begin to recognize who we aren't. It's after we learn who we aren't that the true self emerges. We must first observe which road we don't want to go down before we can see what path we do want to follow. As awareness builds, blind spots reveal themselves and you'll know where to go next on this journey. You might suddenly realize you're judging everyone and everything—especially yourself. You may find yourself being extra defensive in a specific scenario. You may observe that the mind runs completely unchecked during certain activities. Once you become aware of these trends, they will no longer feel natural since you're beginning to see the source of dysfunction. Prolonged intense awareness of your thoughts, coupled with time, will lead to a dramatic improvement in life.

I heard an interviewee on the podcast say that quitting drinking can be the one domino that knocks all the others down. I love this line and fully agree. However, imagine a straight line of dominos that spans the distance of a basketball court. If we quit drinking, we tip over the domino at half court. Cool, but that still leaves the other half of the dominos standing. If we are able to address the protective personality, ego and the thinking mind (we start through awareness), we have the ability to knock ALL the dominos down.

Saddle up

☐ Sit down in a quiet place and become aware of your thoughts as the observer. Don't label them as good or bad.

☐ Once you feel an uncomfortable emotion, use the mind to locate it in the body and place all your awareness onto that area. Breathe into this area with love and compassion. Repeat this process until this becomes a habit.

☐ Instead of asking yourself who you are, ask yourself who you aren't.

☐ Is there a time of day, or during a specific activity where the mind runs completely unchecked? Why do you think this is? Be aware of the types of thoughts that emerge.

The biggest opportunity in your life

If I were to write my own 12 Steps, this would be Step One. Quitting drinking is a once in a lifetime opportunity: embrace it for what it is and ask yourself if you're going to take it. Normal drinkers, who have their own unique set of problems, don't have the opportunity to unfuck themselves like we do. It's of paramount importance we view this entire journey for what it actually is—an opportunity and not a sacrifice. Feel free to jot this one down and put it on Post-it notes in every room of the house. This isn't a Jedi mind trick, but a simple fact. Unfortunately, this mindset is missed by many who embark into an AF life and most view alcohol as something they will be forever giving up or sacrificing. They go through life with the constant hum of what they "can't" do (drink) and completely miss everything they can do without the toxin alcohol. This then creates a mindset of lack, or that something is missing in life, resulting in an underlying mood of pessimism. Someone who has quit drinking and views this new lifestyle as a sacrifice or that they can no longer do something (drink) is called a dry drunk. Another characteristic of a dry drunk is someone whose AF plan consists of one thing: not drinking. In addition, when we view an AF life as if we are "missing out" on something, we start experiencing addiction whackamole, and addictions start presenting themselves in other aspects of life.

If we embrace this crossroads in life as an opportunity, you may find yourself waking up before the alarm clock goes off ready to get a head start on the day. You might say to yourself, "You know, I'm full of anxiety right now, but I'm gonna ride this one out without drinking because I know better times are ahead." You'll go from having the fear of missing out (FOMO) to the joy of missing out (JOMO). Getting shitfaced at your friend Mindy's bachelorette party for three nights straight in your mid-thirties? No thanks. Take a trip to Italy, learn how to salsa dance, or start playing the bass guitar. This is the focal point behind Allen Carr's *The Easy Way to Stop Drinking*, and then Annie Grace does a remarkable job of taking this idea to the next level in her book *This Naked Mind*.

With this mindset, you'll start to look at things in a more advantageous fashion, that life is working in your favor. For example, if some of your friends initially congratulate you on your decision to quit drinking but begin to fade away in your life, you'll recognize that this is a chance to build healthier relationships with new people. You may arrive at a moment in your journey where you have no clue what you like to do in life. Do a quick Google search of "new hobbies" or "fun things to do" and you've got about 78 years' worth of exciting activities. This again is another example of the reverse order of how recovery works. We must first allow people, places and things to depart from our lives before space is created for new ones to enter. Want to be a professional cartographer? In sobriety, you've got that opportunity. Want to be the loving mother you've always wanted to be? Go for it! Financially, you've got an incredible opportunity ahead of you as well. According to the Recovery Elevator sobriety tracker, I've saved over 55k in the past 4.5 years. This is the reason I was able to buy a kickass house on 1.5 acres near the foothills just outside beautiful Bozeman, Montana. Ben and I love the epic sunsets!

Don't beat yourself up if you're not fully embracing this mindset. When I first began this journey on January 1st, 2010, I thought my life was over. I didn't think a girl would ever want to date me again. I thought I was going to be booted out of my fantasy football league (I'm a two-time champ and both league titles came in sobriety. In addition, both drafts took place in Las Vegas and I was the only one not shitfaced while drafting. Coincidence? Not a chance). I thought that when I quit drinking, I would be left with a couple dozen friends on Facebook or have to leave Facebook entirely and return to Myspace where it would just be me and Tom. I seriously believed I was going to become an outcast. I envisioned my tombstone reading,

R.I.P.
Paul Churchill, Born April 10th
Kicked Ass 1982-2010
Moped Around 2010-2074

I've been wrong about many things in life, but I completely missed the mark on predicting how my life would look without alcohol. I was WAY off. So many incredible opportunities have come my way.

Let this perspective sink in over time. Deep inside, your heart and soul already know ditching the booze is an opportunity of a lifetime, but it can take some time for the mind to get up to speed, so be patient. If you're wishing alcohol was still part of your life and you're not feeling overly optimistic about the near future, that's okay. It's completely acceptable and expected to reach points of frustration. It's okay to say "FUCK, life is coming at me in a fierce way right now and a drink would be nice." Don't squash these thoughts and feelings. Be aware of them and simply let them come and allow them to go. Every single emotion known to humankind will eventually pass. Be patient, allow life to unfold and watch the abundance of opportunities present themselves. That's the good news. These opportunities in life will simply show up with more and more frequency the longer we remain AF. You might be saying to yourself, "Okay, I understand this isn't a sacrifice, but I'm not seeing any clear kickass opportunities in front of me." Most likely, several opportunities have already come and gone, and you weren't able to see them due to their being labeled by the thinking mind as 'bad' or 'not a good fit'. That's okay because these opportunities never stop showing up in a life without alcohol. So many opportunities will start showing up where your new motto will be, "If it's not a hell yes, then it's a hell no."

Saddle up

☐ Do you view life without alcohol as an opportunity or a sacrifice?

☐ Do you spend more mental energy thinking of what you can't do in an alcohol-free life instead of what you are now able to do?

☐ How much money do you spend on alcohol in a year? What would you love to spend that on?

☐ Are you able to recognize things working in your favor? For example, when you start seeing old drinking friends less?

Internal vs. External

The bulk of this is an inside job. It always has been and always will be. Most likely you've been regulating your internal state of being with external things such as alcohol, food, people and experiences, to name a few. It's prudent that we don't fall into this same trap while in sobriety. Moderating internal states of discomfort externally is not sustainable. We found this out while drinking and we eventually we'll reach the same conclusion in sobriety if we continue to reach for other substances. In the next chapter we'll cover specific techniques of how to go internal, but at this moment, all we need to do is to become familiar with the idea that inner peace is sourced from within and not from external sources such as alcohol, identities, possessions, experiences, job titles and milestones in life.

The reason why internal growth is more important than external is because we can do some major leap frogging. For example, when we quit drinking, it's important that we fill the void left by alcohol with a supportive community. We have two options here: 1. We can go to countless 12 Step meetings hoping to meet other sober peeps, join sober groups on places like meetup.com, join the Recovery Elevator private community Café RE, ask sober friends for coffee or lunch, or 2. Start building that community within by connecting the body and mind. Once these two have merged, an unshakable internal communal connection has been built that isn't contingent on the external environment.

Now, both options bear fruit and I don't recommend picking one while ignoring the other. However, I highly recommend focusing your efforts within. If we work on building a healthy internal community, the external community solves itself with time. This is a universal law. The quality of the internal connection will be reflected in the outside world and vice versa. Once the body and mind are harmoniously reunited, you'll be vibrating at a higher frequency. These higher vibrational frequencies feel good to be around. Literally, people will "feel good" simply standing next to you. They won't know what's going on, but they'll say to themselves, "I wonder what Richard is doing this weekend." You'll start to receive more text messages. More invites to social events.

Soon you will start to recognize an abundance of community in all aspects of your life.

It's tough to create external tranquility when there's still a disconnection within, which is why it's so important to work on cultivating self-compassion in our inner world. Be patient, this takes time. In early sobriety, it felt like I was jamming every square block into a round hole. This is totally normal. In fact, this transition from external to internal needs to happen slowly. If we were to go from 24 years of daily drinking to 24 hours straight on the meditation cushion, the result might be an emotional explosion. This release of energy and pent-up emotions needs to happen, but we're going to take our time and go slow. We don't want to completely shock the system.

It's important that we focus internally because nothing external is permanent. If we assign happiness to our homes, jobs, significant others, and pets, to name a few, then a trap has been set. What happens when one of these things is taken away? Do we search for replacements? You can see this leads to an endless search for comfort and happiness. I love doing Recovery Elevator, the podcast, the meetups, retreats, etc. It feels like I have the best job in the world, but I have to be careful that I don't attach my sense of identity and happiness to the project. The same thing goes with my Standard Poodle, Ben. The dog is without a doubt man's best friend and Ben is mine. He's been my rock these past five years, my calm and sober sidekick. He's added so much joy to my life, but I recognize that Ben's time will come to an end, most likely well before mine, and I need to be okay without him.

When we first begin this journey, most of us will be clinging to the external world for comfort mostly because it's known. We like predictability, even if it consists of boredom, unhappiness, shame and a shitty job. An intimidating part about turning the gaze inward is that we begin to enter the unknown and this can instantly cause the heart to beat faster. We'll cover trusting this unknown later in the book but from this moment on, I want you to be aware (we're already using the concept from above) of where your efforts and focus are directed. Activities such as yoga and hiking are great because they allow us to go internal and external at the same time.

For probably the first three years away from alcohol, when I encountered an intense emotional charge or life threw a curveball my way, I always went external to mollify the inner turmoil. I would sit on my couch and scan through a list of external activities to make me feel better. Hot springs, go for a run, take a drive, ask a friend out for dinner, go see a movie, go to an A.A. meeting, play ice hockey, etc. Sure, each of these are far better options than drinking and some of them allow for introspection, but most of them are external. And what happens if I have an injury that prevents me from walking or running? Then half of these options are no longer viable.

I remember one day, a little after three years AF, where I was feeling the feels. I was so sick of conjuring up external ways to mitigate my internal discord that I just sat. I didn't do anything. I sat on my couch with Ben. The TV wasn't on, music wasn't playing, my cellphone wasn't in my hand and I just sat. The idea of sitting, alone, without distractions was terrifying to me. This meant there was a good chance that everything I drank to suppress would start drifting to the surface. Even though it had been over 3 years since my last drink, I still didn't let this happen. Every time I felt an uncomfortable emotion,

I would say, "Hey Ben, want to go for a run?" So, I just sat. Deep down, I knew this was going to be the next step in my journey, but I kept fighting it until one day, I took a seat. The word "relax" doesn't come into the picture for quite some time, but after what seemed like eons of restlessness and acute discomfort, I felt a sliver of inner peace for the first time. Also, while sitting, I first became aware of how disconnected my body and mind were. That was the day in my journey where I began consciously connecting the body and mind. Fast forward to the present day, I love sitting. I can sit in any given location and completely lose track of time. There's a park bench about two miles away from my office and, weather permitting, I probably log four to five hours a week on this bench. One of my favorite things to do is sit and watch the sky. Watch clouds form, change shape and create tunnels for airplanes. Watching a

Montana Big Sky sunset on that bench with my dog Ben fills my heart. The more internal I go, the more wholeness and inner peace I experience.

Saddle up

☐ Do you see ways you've been regulating your internal state of being with external substances and activities? Can you think of other ways than alcohol?

☐ On a piece of paper, make two lists, writing down the internal and external strategies you are using.

☐ Are you able to sit for long periods of time and relax? What would that feel like?

☐ Do you experience inner peace?

You can't do this alone.

There are several gray areas in recovery, but this isn't one of them. This one is black and white. We cannot do this alone, even though it's how most people's journey into an AF life begins. If we are to be successful in this endeavor through the long term, we eventually will find ourselves surrounded by dozens of loving people—both in recovery and not—who are aware of our goal of moving forward in life without alcohol. I know this sounds scary, but it's a beautiful thing. In time, your heart will lead you here. Don't worry, we'll go slow with this one.

I began my journey solo and I imagine you did the same. Almost every person I've interviewed on the podcast starts alone. Eventually, after getting our asses repeatedly kicked by alcohol, we reach a tipping point where we start on-boarding support. Most likely the order looks something like this: conscious internal reflection, usually after a shitty moment involving alcohol, a Google search, a self-help book, blog or podcast, a friend, therapist, a doctor, a family member, significant other, then an in person community comprised of both people who don't drink and normal drinkers. Why don't we leapfrog directly from internal gazing to the supportive community? Well, some do, and I hope this book can give you the boost needed, but most of us follow a similar path and there are several reasons for this.

A drinking problem is most likely the first dilemma you've encountered in life that you haven't been able to successfully think yourself out of. The reason for this is that the conscious and unconscious mind are asking two different questions. Consciously, you're asking "How can I control my drinking, or how do I quit altogether?" The more powerful unconscious mind is asking "What's the quickest and most effective way to regulate inner discomfort?" and its best solution for quite some time has been alcohol. You may have a Harvard degree, but that doesn't mean shit when it comes to quitting drinking. It's extremely hard to get a memo to the part of the mind that is running 95% of the show: the subconscious. The thinking mind first must exhaust every solution we can think of and the bulk of these are usually silly moderation techniques such as 'no drinks before 5 pm', 'no more hard alcohol' and telling yourself you'll never drink alone. The brain thinks of geographical cures, in hopes that a new location or setting will curb the drinking. My mind convinced me my drinking was going to stay in Spain after I walked away from the bar. The mind got me again when I moved to Seattle for grad school. The drinking followed me both times. Perhaps you're working in an industry where alcohol is part of the culture and you think changing jobs will help (after doing the podcast for over four years, I'm convinced alcohol is intermingled with every work environment apart from the rehab industry). Eventually we reach a point where we realize that not only have our ideas not worked, but they've landed us in the position we find ourselves in. This is a powerful moment in everyone's journey because it's when we start thinking outside of the box or relying less on thoughts and ideas.

Another reason we embark on the biggest journey in our lives alone is because of the stigma. I'm a firm believer that the stigma is more lethal than the drug alcohol itself. I thought the planets would fall out of orbit if I told another human being about my drinking. It's the stigma that forces us to go through the muck of addiction for much longer than necessary. Even though I was paying a therapist over a hundred dollars an hour, I still lied to her about my drinking. I was okay with her thinking I was a sad, depressed and anxious human being, but no way did I want her to think I was an alcoholic. What's worse is that the stigma is completely fabricated (Thank you, Big Alcohol and the 80s "Just Say No" campaign.) 99% of people want you to be the happiest and healthiest version of you. The other 1% are assholes and you don't need them in your life anyways. Moving into an AF life has the ability to remove all the toxic people in your life within a matter of months. It's important to "let" this tailwind unfold and allow these people to leave your life. What usually happens is that eventually we reach a point where the pain caused by alcohol is greater than the imagined pain we'll face when we tell others about our drinking.

We also reach a point where we're sick of making false statements to ourselves. Do any of these statements sound familiar?

- "I don't have an issue with drinking."

- "I'll quit drinking after New Year's."
- "Once work settles down, I'll cut down on the rum and Cokes."
- "I'm only going to drink on the weekends."
- "No more drinking alone."
- "This will be my last drink for the rest of my life."

Every single non-negotiable line in the sand is crossed and this is flat out exhausting. Internally, we deliver a shit ton of promises we fail to keep, and this is demoralizing. We begin to see this insanity and shortly after, clarity enters in the form of short durations of honesty. Once this honesty and trust within reaches a certain level, we peacefully say, "Fuck, I think it's time for a second opinion." Another huge step forward has been taken. We realize that what we have been doing on the individual level isn't working and we start asking others what worked for them.

We then ask for help. Whoa…. I know. This is SCARY. Most likely, it's been a long time since you've reached out for support for anything, let alone drinking. For many, asking for help may be one of the hardest parts of this journey. Seriously, we are terrible at asking for help. Like 2017 Cleveland Browns bad. Eventually there will come a time when we take off the pride hat and say, "I can't do this alone; I need help." Another huge step forward has been made.

I know reading this section may have been tough, but I've got great news. Doing this journey with others is fun and it's what your heart has been pulling for all along. There is so much camaraderie in an AF life. Get ready to forge some of the most intense relationships in your life. If you ever attend a Recovery Elevator retreat; you may find yourself talking about your rock bottom minutes after meeting somebody for the first time, and it's going to feel great. I can almost guarantee you that your heart will bloom within the first 48 hours and often much sooner. The heart knows exactly what it's doing and it's so much fun to watch people come online and be the true versions of themselves in a matter of minutes at these retreats. If we fully embrace the pure, inevitable fact that we can't do this alone, chaos starts sliding into order.

Saddle up

- ☐ Do you think you can do this alone?
- ☐ Have you tried to do this alone? Has it worked?
- ☐ Do you have trouble asking for help? Why do you think this is? Is there a time in your life that you asked for help and you didn't receive it?
- ☐ Imagine being able to sit with someone who knows what you are struggling with. How does that feel?
- ☐ Visualize a support team that has got your back. Write down every member of this team, in all areas.

Knowledge and Willpower Alone Won't Cut It

On the afternoon of January 1st, 2010, I went to Barnes & Noble in the Seattle Northgate Mall with a crushing hangover, and pulled a book titled *Beyond the Influence* by Katherine Ketchum off the shelf. I looked over both shoulders to make sure nobody saw that I was reading a self-help book about alcohol addiction and I started to read. As the song "Fireflies" from Owl City piped through Barnes & Noble, I began to fill my brain with knowledge about alcohol. Armed with information about how dangerous alcohol can be for the body and mind and using strategies for how to remain AF, coupled with intense willpower, I went nearly two and a half years without alcohol. After the initial withdrawal from alcohol and an uncomfortable thirty or so days where it felt like I was learning to walk again,

I started overall to feel better. And after a couple months, I felt great. A feeling of bliss, which had been absent since my early twenties came back and I was riding a pink cloud which lasted nearly a year. The fact that my emotional state had dramatically improved in such a short period of time reinforced that alcohol was shit. Only when I completely removed the toxin ethanol from my body was I able to see how it was physically and mentally holding me back. I experienced mental clarity, bothersome physical ailments disappeared, inflammation in the body decreased and at about five months AF, I looked in the mirror and saw a six pack in my stomach starting to emerge. So much mental bandwidth was freed up because I no longer had to figure out when to drink, how much to drink, when to stop, what days to take off, how to mitigate shame the next morning, etc. I had no idea how much energy alcohol was sucking out of every aspect of my life until it was completely removed. Life started to get good and removing alcohol from my life was the reason.

I remember being asked by a friend while in graduate school at the University of Washington in the summer of 2010 if I would ever drink again. I unequivocally, resolutely said "No, never again." I'm a smart enough guy with unrivaled willpower and there was no way I was ever going to drink again. Heads up, high levels of willpower can backfire like it did for me because it prolongs the solo journey. People with sports backgrounds, like I have, often have the "no pain, no gain" mentality and they think that they all alone, with steadfast determination, can overcome this problem.

In the summer of 2012, my willpower, which is an exhaustible and finite resource, ran out. Looking back, it's clear what happened. The knowledge acquired in early 2010 gave me the motivation to depart from alcohol, and then I used willpower as my only source of fuel. For two and a half years, I was looking at sobriety as a sacrifice and not an opportunity. This mindset of lack—that something was missing in life—wasn't sustainable and eventually I drank again.

I don't want to downplay the importance of knowledge. It's a big step forward when we start doing research about alcohol and what it's doing to our bodies and minds, but this isn't about what you know, but what you do. The knowledge acquired on this journey is secondary to action and comes with limitations. Knowledge alone isn't enough because it stays in the brain and doesn't make it to the heart and soul where the disconnection resides. No amount of knowledge will nourish and sustain your heart. It can never bring you ultimate happiness or peace. Much more than knowledge is required on this journey. This journey requires intense introspection and energy.

On page 39 of the *Big Book of Alcoholics Anonymous*, it says, "The actual or potential alcoholic will be absolutely unable to stop drinking on the basis of self-knowledge." This idea has been around for quite some time now. These dry drunks are in a constant state of unease because something is always missing: alcohol. They've never truly said goodbye. If you've been away from alcohol for several months and it still feels as if you're living life in the dentist chair, then this could be an indicator you're relying too much on knowledge and willpower on this journey.

The biggest reason why knowledge alone isn't enough, is that it's usually based on fear. I think all self-help alcohol addiction books serve a purpose but beware the ones that use fear as a primary motivator. My goal is to inspire readers to quit drinking because a much better life awaits, and not because dreadful things will happen if they continue to drink. It's important to understand that alcohol is dangerous and lethal shit that can wreak havoc on the drinker and those around them, but this should constitute only a fraction of the motivation for why you've made the decision to quit drinking. Fear can tip the scales and push someone into an AF life, but it won't be sustainable. I've interviewed several people on the podcast that have been told by a medical professional that if they continue to drink, the health consequences will be dire. Nearly all of them drank again. In Episode 56, I interview Bill who was told that if he drinks again, the result will likely be death. I'll let Bill take it from here.

I had been a successful "functional alcoholic," drinking nearly every day almost all of my adult life. My liver enzymes had always been elevated from my drinking, but they got so high in 2010 that my doctor ordered a liver biopsy which revealed the onset of irreversible cirrhosis of the liver. He said, "You have to stop drinking or you are headed to an early grave." The fear motivated me to quit that day cold-turkey. As powerful as fear is, it has its limits. Eventually my fear and willpower, which was all I had in my toolkit, subsided. My addiction convinced me that I could cut back from the fifth of whisky I used to drink to just a few shots a day. I started "moderate" drinking again and then after just a few months I was back to my fifth a day.

—Bill, Gettysburg, PA

Fortunately, Bill eventually did quit drinking and has remained alcohol-free since September 2015.

If you embarked on this journey alone and are using willpower as your primary source of sobriety fuel, don't beat yourself up. That's how I started. There is no single correct pathway to take. It's all part of the process. I'm hoping to simply give you some ideas and expedite the process.

Saddle up

☐ Ask yourself where you habitually look to willpower when making decisions.

☐ Do you notice that you have less willpower at the end of a day?

☐ Is knowledge a primary source of fuel for you on this journey?

An AF life isn't forever, it's just for today.

At the time of writing this chapter it has been 1,642 days since my last drink. Will I go the rest of my life without drinking? I'd like to hope so, but who knows? The thought of doing anything for the rest of my life, be it twenty pushups a day, being the best version of me, not drinking, etc., makes my heart rate rise, which is why I don't think about it. When I first started writing this book I was completely overwhelmed by the task. It's basically 250 podcast episodes in 4 months. Yikes. But once I looked at it as one letter, one word, one sentence at a time, one chapter at a time, I felt the stress lift and the process of writing a book became manageable, even enjoyable. It's the same thing with this journey. There is no shortage of clichés, mantras and sayings in recovery, but the most important one is, 'One day at a time.'

If the thought of not having a glass of champagne at your wedding or retirement party is causing something to stir inside, then don't think about it. I imagine that wondering if you'll have enough money in your bank account for retirement will also provoke anxiety. You're not there yet. If you find yourself wondering how in the hell you're going to attend a bachelor or bachelorette party sober, let alone address the questions of why you're not drinking, stop thinking about it. You're not there yet. The protective personality wants you to run every possible scenario in your head weeks, months and years before an event arrives. When we find ourselves constantly living in the future, trying to navigate multiple scenarios where alcohol will be present, of course anxiety spikes. 99.9% of those scenarios will never happen, so stop thinking about them. If you're blowing your circuits asking yourself how you're going to make it thirty days and you're on day one, stop asking. The mind isn't equipped to cope with future events that haven't arrived yet, let alone with the end of the day. With compassion, remind yourself to bring the mental projections back to today. If the edge of life becomes particularly sharp, tell yourself one minute at a time, or thirty seconds at a time. This five-word teaching is a hint of something much more robust; the present moment. In fact, I recommend changing one day at a time (ODAAT) to one moment at a time (OMAAT). Making this shift will have a profound impact on your life.

At first, living OMAAT can be extremely difficult and takes practice. If you find yourself wondering how to do this, keep in mind you are constantly surrounded by Zen masters that you can learn from in the form of cats, dogs, trees, flowers, and basically every other living organism on the planet. Human beings are one of the few species on the planet that gets ulcers for this very reason; we are rarely in the present moment and constantly find ourselves ruminating on the past or future. If I could ask my Standard Poodle Ben what time it is, he wouldn't understand the question and would look at me and say, "Come on, Paul, Standard Poodles are smart, but we're not that smart, this has to be a trick question because obviously the time is now. It's the only time it can be." Our pets can teach us so much. Nearly every other species on the planet is firmly grounded in the present moment. The incessant departure from the present moment causes so much unnecessary human suffering. This may seem easy, but as English novelist George Orwell said, "To see what's right in front of our noses requires a constant struggle."

OMAAT brings us to the only place happiness can exist—right now. The only time that a deep inner peace that isn't contingent on external matters can take place is now. This is why the concept of "hope" is a delicate matter. Don't get me wrong, having hope is great, but keep in mind that hope is always located in the future. If you're always hoping to one day be happy, you'll never be happy because you're hoping for something that always lives in the future and which is never in the now. The only time it's ever been possible to be happy is right now. Let that sink in for a second. It's now or never.

When this journey gets difficult, no matter how hard the mind tries to pull you towards a future event, do your best to stay in this moment. According to Eckhart Tolle in *The Power of Now*, "As soon as you honor the present moment, all unhappiness and struggle dissolve and life begins to flow with joy and ease." This is why the allure of extreme sports is so strong, because it pulls people into the present moment. If an extreme base jumper, wearing a squirrel suit with fabric for wings, departs from the present moment for a split second, the result could be death. We can see why high intensity sports such as football, skiing, hockey, basketball, even ping pong, to name a few, can be so enjoyable because we find ourselves wholly, if temporarily, in the present moment. Do your absolute best to pull yourself back into the present moment when you become aware the mind is reliving the past or navigating the future. This is another way to dramatically improve your life.

Saddle up

☐ How does it feel when you think about going AF the rest of your life? How about when it's just for a day? Can you give yourself permission to focus on today?

☐ What does ODAAT mean for you?

☐ What are some events in the future you've been worrying about? Can you let go of these worries for now?

☐ What is a doomsday scenario you've unnecessarily created and run with? What are the facts? What is hypothetical?

☐ Do you agree that the only time happiness can exist is now?

There is nothing fundamentally wrong with you.

Let me say that again. There is nothing wrong with you at the core level. I already know this much about you and I want you to start believing the same because deep down you know it's true. You weren't brought into this universe missing a certain set of neurological circuits that are preventing you from being happy or living a normal life. There is nothing that was left undone or omitted upon your creation. You already possess everything needed to initiate the healing your heart and soul have been longing for all along. You may be vehemently disagreeing with this and you might have notes from medical professionals indicating otherwise, but trust me, if you go down this path long enough you'll reach a point where you'll say, "Damn, that Paul Churchill guy was on to something, the answer has been inside all along." On top of that, you'll reach another point where you'll realize nothing is intrinsically wrong with you, nothing needs to change and you're perfect just the way you are.

From 1998 to 2017, I took thirteen different meds in tablet form to fix something that I was told was wrong with me or out of chemical balance. These included Paxil, Celexa, Lexapro, Prozac, Zoloft, Abilify, Cymbalta, Lithium, Lamictal, Benzodiazepines, Strattera, Ritalin and Vynanse. I was diagnosed with bipolar disorders I and II, anxiety disorders, unipolar depression, acute attention deficit disorder, and a laundry list of other disorders and syndromes that are all bullshit. After nearly two decades on a cocktail of Big Pharma's best creations, I started to question the efficacy of these medications. In Episode 118, titled "The Black Dog," I talk about the depression I was experiencing at the time and a listener forwarded me a Joe Rogan podcast with former psychiatrist Kelly Brogan. Dr. Brogan talks about how she put down her prescription pad because she was questioning if she was doing more harm than good with prescribing psychotropic drugs. She also mentions a book titled *The Anatomy of an Epidemic* by Robert Whitaker, which sets off to answer the question of why there are currently more people than ever on disability with mental illnesses if there have been so many magic bullet scientific breakthroughs with mental health. Let's just say this was an eye-opening read, and in the fall of 2017, I tapered first off my antidepressant, followed by my ADHD meds. Yes, this was an extremely rough couple of months. (And for the record, please don't taper off these meds without medical supervision. Big Pharma won't tell you this, but these are incredibly difficult meds to stop taking.) But it allowed me to come back online and feel again. I'm significantly happier off antidepressants and I'm able to focus way better without ADHD meds.

I don't want to go too far down the rabbit hole of the efficacy of psychotropic meds but Robert Whitaker debunks the chemical imbalance theory which has been widely propagated by Big Pharma to fill prescriptions since the release of Prozac in 1987. I'm sure many readers, including myself, have been told by a physician or psychiatrist that there is a chemical imbalance in the brain that can be corrected with psychotropic medications such as antidepressants. This theory that a certain group of individuals have a biological chemical imbalance simply isn't correct. Although it is true that people have different levels of serotonin and other chemicals in the brain, a correlation between certain levels of serotonin and depression has yet to be found. Some people with low serotonin levels report high levels of happiness, while others with high levels of serotonin can find themselves depressed.

At this moment, you may be having difficulty believing there is nothing wrong with you at your core. That a small imperfection didn't exist while you rested in your mother's womb. That's okay. As you continue to read, I want you to tell yourself the truth—that you're perfect the way you are—because deep down you already know this, and the truth is starting to emerge.

Saddle up

☐ Do you think there is something wrong with you?

☐ Do you feel you were born with all the components needed to be whole?

☐ What do you think of the chemical imbalance theory? Do you feel a chemical imbalance has played a role in your addiction?

☐ Are you perfect just the way you are?

Is life possible after alcohol?

Not only is life after alcohol possible but, as long as you keep the protective personality in check and stay away from the booze, life will continue to improve indefinitely. I'm not going to kid you, there will be some intense learning curves and the desire to jump back into your old way of life may be strong at times, but there are countless plateau moments on this journey that make it all worth it. Internally, spring is right around the corner and you're like a flower right on the precipice of blooming after a long winter. Some of the anxiety you've experienced is simply being excited about the next chapter of your life. You've been anxiously waiting for quite some time for this next part of your life to begin.

One amazing thing that awaits you in an AF life is authentic connection with people. You'll have the capacity to deepen the bonds with everyone in your life and the most important relationship that you will strengthen is the one with yourself. You'll find yourself having fewer surface-level conversations because you're able to go much deeper. Interest in social media newsfeeds will decrease because you'll start to see the shallowness in them.

There's a lot of life to live after alcohol and more people than ever are starting to recognize this. There is a sober movement taking place across the planet and you're a trailblazer in this movement. Our society has been yearning for places to connect and build altruistic relationships with other human beings without alcohol and there are more opportunities now than ever. It wasn't long ago that your best option to connect with others who didn't drink alcohol took place in a church basement, but there are more sober events now than ever.

In 2018, the pop/hip-hop star Macklemore headlined the first ever "Recovery Fest" in Rhode Island and in March of 2019, the first "Sober by Southwest," a spinoff of the massive South by Southwest music conference in Austin, Texas, took place. Sponsors were lining up to be part of this event, and when the originators of South by Southwest first heard of its alcohol-free counterpart, their response was, "We understand exactly why this event is so needed." There is a company called Daybreaker that hosts alcohol-free raves and some of these high energy dance parties take place before work.

There are now even sober bars such as Sans Bar, which is a sober pop-up bar in Austin, Texas, that is on a national tour across the country. At first, these sober establishments showed up in larger markets such as London and New York City, but now they can be found in cities of all sizes. Normal drinkers are also seeking social interactions that aren't primarily based around alcohol.

In 2018, I started a group called Sober is Sexy on meetup.com and the response was surprising. Since Bozeman, MT, is a relatively small town, I recognized several of the names who joined the alcohol-free group. I initially expected the group to be comprised of people who don't drink, but more than half of the group's members did. After asking a couple members why they joined a sober group even though they drank, they all responded with something like how they wanted to meet people in a setting that didn't involve drunken baboons.

What is possible in a life without alcohol? Anything you want. Seriously, anything is possible in an AF life. The most important thing that is possible in an AF life is happiness. Actually, I should correct myself—it's not happiness, because that has an inverse called sadness. What awaits you in a life without alcohol is joy. This is an inner peace that never waivers despite what others think about you or what is happening in your current life situation. Joy is the holy grail in life.

Saddle up

☐ Next time you catch yourself with anxiety, do a body check for your physical symptoms. Is it possible that you have mislabeled your excitement as anxiety? (these symptoms can be similar…)

☐ Write down several detailed elements of your future life without alcohol. Be as specific and sensory as possible, including locations, emotions, people and experiences.

☐ What makes you nervous about what awaits you in an AF life?

☐ What do you *really* want in a life without alcohol?

Focus on the similarities and not the differences.

On a Tuesday in August 2012, I attended my first A.A. meeting to support a friend who was questioning her drinking. At that time, it had been two and a half years since my last drink and the thought of taking a drink was the last thing on my mind. I was drunk two days later. During this meeting, I heard stories of multiple DUIs, divorce, bankruptcy, prison terms, hospitalizations and more. As the meeting progressed, the idea that perhaps I didn't have a drinking problem because my history didn't include this wreckage begin to emerge. After that meeting, I left ecstatic because I was fully convinced that I didn't have a drinking problem and I hit the town two days later. At 2:30 a.m. early Friday morning, after coming home from the bars and drinking all my roommate's alcohol, probably 20+ drinks for the evening, I found myself at the computer googling if it was safe to drink rubbing alcohol or hydrogen peroxide, which is all I had left in the house and I couldn't buy alcohol past 2 a.m. in Montana. Fuck me, that got ugly fast. What in the hell just happened? I woke up the next morning feeling awful and completely defeated but I learned a valuable lesson, which was that my previous decision to quit drinking had been the correct one.

What happened is that I was so eager to distance myself from what an "alcoholic" looked like—thank you, stigma—that I was completely focusing on the subtle details that would set me apart from everyone in that meeting. I also found myself doing the same thing when I was fully ready to quit drinking in 2014 by telling myself that A.A. can't work for me because I'm not like anyone in this room. This terminal uniqueness is dangerous because it places you on a lonely island of isolation where the solar system orbits around you.

If you find yourself in a 12 Step meeting, SMART, Refuge or any other recovery meeting, focus on the pain and circumstances that led you to that meeting and not what hasn't happened to you… yet. In 2012, when I attended my first A.A. meeting, I didn't have a DUI on my record yet, but I fixed that in the summer of 2014.

The mind will do its best to convince you that you're particularly special and you're not like anyone else. Sure, your name is Susy, from Grand Rapids, MI, you don't like Brussels sprouts, and you're allergic to cats, and therefore none of the text in this book can apply to you. Of course, everyone has a different set of backgrounds and particular circumstances and experiences, but after interviewing over 250 guests on the podcast, nearly everyone's stories follow similar trajectories. This is why the camaraderie on this journey is so strong. If you ever attend a Recovery Elevator retreat, you'll find yourself saying, "No way, that happened to me too," multiple times.

As you read, be aware of when the thinking mind tries to distance yourself from the very people that have already walked this path and could be of vital assistance in your journey. Focusing on these differences will prevent you from leaning into the most important resource on this journey—community.

Saddle up

☐ When and how have you told yourself you don't have a drinking problem because you don't fit the stereotype?

☐ When while reading this book have you made a case for why you're different?

What is recovery?

This may come as a shock to you, since it's part of the podcast title (Recovery Elevator), but I'm not fully on board with the word recovery, especially when we use it in its progressive form to describe someone who no longer drinks: a recovering alcoholic. The definition for what an alcoholic looks like is already confusing so by adding the word "recovering" in front of it, it adds another layer of complexity. What exactly are we recovering from? An addiction to alcohol? Past traumas that alcohol has been used to cover up? Are we hoping to recover something that is missing in life? Is recovery a lifelong endeavor?

There are several definitions of recovery, but I like Russell Brand's the best when he says we are recovering the person we were intended to be. Recovery describes the time in our lives when we decide to follow the guidance of the heart and soul to find authentic altruistic internal and external connection as it was always intended. Recovery isn't about getting back on the right path, but about embracing the path we currently find ourselves on and learning the lessons we are supposed to learn.

Can we ever fully recover? Absolutely. The authors of the book *Alcoholics Anonymous* believed so as well. They use the past tense of the word recover (recovered) in the *Big Book* over twenty times, which is something that most members of A.A. miss. In fact, in Episode 212 of the Recovery Elevator podcast, I talk about how this is the most controversial word in A.A. You rarely hear the word "recovered" in A.A. meetings and when you do, there is a shift in energy in the room and people begin to get uncomfortable. This is because it challenges an identity, and the majority of attendees think meetings, recovery, sponsorship, etc. are for life. Weekly and sometimes daily meetings may be for some, but it doesn't have to be for everyone.

Will we be in recovery the remainder of our lives? Yes and no. For one, we can always deepen with inner peace, wholeness and connection. On the other hand, there will come a time when we have fully recovered from alcohol and we need to start *being* the loving joyful person we were always intended to be. At this moment in my journey, I feel I have recovered from alcohol. I no longer think about drinking in social situations, when I'm feeling lonely, am stressed, or I am feeling anxious. Alcohol is no longer a coping mechanism in my life.

Saddle up

☐ Do you think a "recovering alcoholic" can ever fully recover and become recovered?

☐ What are you trying to recover that alcohol took from you?

☐ What do you think recovery is? Who is the person you were meant to be?

The Word Alcoholic

I think that a bunch of terms/descriptors used to describe addiction and the healing process need to be completely thrown out. The unconscious mind already has a preset idea, thanks to the stigma of what an "alcoholic" is supposed to look like and once you identify with that, well, the unconscious can take over. I have officially broken up with the word alcoholic and I encourage you to do so as well. I'm not saying to shy away from the fact you may have a drinking problem, but don't identify with the label alcoholic because the unconscious mind already has a full set of negative descriptors that it will then attach itself to if you label yourself as an alcoholic. The word alcoholic is the ultimate descriptor, and this isn't the case for other diseases such as cancer. When we use the word alcoholic to describe someone, it usually ends the sentence. For example, my neighbor Mike is an alcoholic. Period. When describing someone who has cancer, for example, their disease isn't what fully describes them. For example, my mom has stage four cancer and is the most loving and creative person on the planet. If my mom was an alcoholic, people would probably say, Paul's mom is an alcoholic...period. Something positive rarely comes after the word alcoholic. We don't use the terms cigaretteaholic, methaholic, or gymaholic, so here is my official vote to ditch the word alcoholic because I feel it does more harm than good. When someone decides to stop drinking poison, we shouldn't give them a label that carries a negative charge. Instead, we should come together and celebrate that person's decision to be the best version of the themselves. Here are some other words that come to mind when describing someone who has a drinking problem and has the courage to quit drinking: badass, trailblazer, rock star, leader, straight up gangsta…. You get the point.

Saddle up

☐ What do you think of the word alcoholic?

☐ Do you think the word alcoholic accurately describes someone with a drinking problem?

☐ Do you consider yourself an alcoholic?

Rock Bottoms

I received an email from a listener who said she didn't know if she was ready to quit drinking because she hasn't had what she perceived as a true rock bottom moment yet, such as a DUI, loss of a job due to drinking, or divorce. There is a false understanding that we need to experience a treacherous and obvious rock bottom before we can depart from alcohol. For some this may be true, but most people who quit drinking alcohol reach a moment where they are simply sick and tired of being sick and tired. The voice in the gut, intuition, becomes louder and eventually you realize that today, not the forever promised tomorrow, is the day the journey begins. Keep in mind, all rock bottoms are relative, and your rock bottom moment might come after being late to work for the fifth time while someone else's rock bottom moment may come in a courtroom.

It's important to keep in mind that all rock bottoms happen for our benefit. They are there to teach us whatever we need to learn in life at that moment and usually this lesson is that we should probably quit drinking. A rock bottom moment which is equivalent to the degree of an addiction will inevitably present itself once the conscious and subconscious are on the same page about removing alcohol from our lives. Sometimes we miss the message, which is okay because the universe will always, within time, present us with a clearer lesson. If we don't recognize these rock bottom moments as messages or cues for change from the universe, they will undoubtedly grow in amplitude. They initially start as internal emotional pangs that grow until they manifest in the physical and external world where others can see as well. Once we recognize the true purpose of a rock bottom, we depart from the "Why is this happening to me?" victim mentality and understand the circumstance is happening "for me." If you find yourself in a Frank the Tank moment, streaking towards the quad, just keep in mind, it's all happening for your benefit!

There is a rock bottom moment we cannot come back from and that is death. This is the only line we cross in addiction that we cannot come back from. Unfortunately, if we continue to ignore first the internal and then the external cues, this is where addiction can lead. Again, I want to keep this book positive and uplifting, but it would be irresponsible of me to leave this out. Keep in mind, every rock bottom moment is there to help us, not hurt us. As poet Sade Andria Zabala says, "I understood myself only after I destroyed myself. And only in the process of fixing myself did I know who I really was."

Saddle up

☐ Have you had a rock bottom moment? More than one? What were they? Are they getting worse?

☐ Do you think these rock bottoms are here to help us? Do you think rock bottom moments are necessary? Have you told yourself you don't have a problem with alcohol because you haven't experienced an obvious or clear rock bottom?

Not Everyone is Kung Fu Fighting

Every time I hear the 70s classic "Kung Fu Fighting" by Carl Douglas, I assume that everyone involved is Kung Fu fighting and kicking major ass; after all, the chorus says, "everybody was Kung Fu fighting," as in EVERYBODY. However, I did some investigation and after watching the original music video, which one would assume would be a nonstop frenzy of swift jabs and roundhouses, I was surprised to find that for the most part, nobody was Kung Fu fighting.

I consistently hear the narrative, "You don't understand what it's like to grow up in _____ (insert any town, village, city, district, state, country), all there is to do is drink." Big Alcohol wants us to believe that everyone drinks, all the time, 24/7 and this simply isn't true. According to the 2015 National Survey on Drug Use and Health (NSDUH), 70.1% of American adults reported that they drank the past year; 56% percent reported that they drank in the past month. If you think you'll become the first person on earth who doesn't drink, keep in mind, nearly a third of the people on this planet don't touch the shit.

In addition to thinking everyone has a cocktail permanently glued to their hands, we assume everyone drinks as much as we do. The Pareto Law states that "the top 20 percent of buyers for most any consumer product account for fully 80 percent of sales." The rule can be applied to everything from hair care products to X-Boxes but when it comes to alcohol, it is estimated the top 5% of buyers account for 95% of sales. Big Alcohol is well aware of this which is why they aren't doing much to curb irresponsible drinking.

So, while embarking upon this journey there are two important things to keep in mind: 1. Not everybody is drinking Sea Breezes at the all-inclusive resort in Mexico and 2. Those who are, probably are having 1-2 drinks. Not only are there roughly 2.5 billion people on the planet who don't drink in a given year, but 95% of drinkers don't drink as much as I did, or even close. Oh yeah, one more thing. Those who do drink, give zero fucks if you don't drink. Seriously, they don't care at all. If you do find yourself worrying about a future situation where you think you'll be judged for being the only person at the event not drinking, please stop, because it's a waste of mental energy. Not only are we ruminating about a future event, we are playing out scenarios that will NEVER happen. Calm down. :)

Saddle up

☐ Have you ever told yourself that everyone drinks, and that you'd be the only person who doesn't drink?

☐ Do you think others drink as much as you do?

☐ Are you concerned about what others will think about you if you're not drinking?

Recovery isn't black or white. There are many pathways leading to the same place.

When I first began this journey, I thought it was A.A. or bust and there was a particular path that I needed to follow in order to successfully quit drinking, but that's not the case. There is no right or wrong way to do this and according to Lance Dodes in *The Sober Truth*, most people get sober outside of A.A. and don't receive any formal treatment. This has been coined as "spontaneous sobriety." What works for someone else may not work for you and it's encouraged to dabble in several arenas of recovery before selecting a path that feels right for you. It is also important to constantly change things up. A.A. isn't for everyone, but before you reach this conclusion, don't fully write off the program after one or two meetings.

There are several recovery programs such SMART Recovery, Refuge Recovery, Life Ring, SOS (Secular Organizations for Sobriety), Women for Sobriety, to name a few, and there are countless recovery blogs, online support communities and recovery podcasts such as Recovery Happy Hour, The Recovery Revolution and That Sober Guy Podcast.

My journey led me to plant medicine (ayahuasca) at nearly four years of sobriety, and some vehemently tried to tell me why this was wrong, that this isn't what recovery is "supposed" to look like. If someone tells you that your recovery approach is unconventional or wrong, this has nothing to do with you. It is simply control issues on display from the other person. I don't recommend voicing this but keep it in mind. Someone said that I was the most fucked-up person in recovery for doing ayahuasca. This same person later did ayahuasca…. and hasn't drank since.

You, and only you, know what's best for your journey and do your best to quiet the external noise. If your journey isn't headed in the right direction, the body and external environment will always, without fail, let you know.

Saddle up

☐ Do you think there is a blueprint of what recovery is supposed to look like?

☐ Has someone told you that your approach is wrong? How did you feel about that?

☐ Have you explored alternative treatments that are outside the norm?

☐ Have you found yourself being critical of someone else's approach to an alcohol-free life?

Tracking Alcohol-Free Time

I used to start each episode of the podcast with, "Welcome to the Recovery Elevator podcast, my name is Paul Churchill and thank you for joining us. According to the Recovery Elevator sobriety tracker, I have been sober for ___ (number of days)." I have stopped doing this for several reasons. Don't get me wrong, going nearly 1,700+ days without a drink at the time of writing this is a huge accomplishment, and it's important we all celebrate sobriety milestones, but I realized a sneaky trap had been set. I was placing too much importance and self-worth on a clock. I was too focused on quantity, not quality and what would happen if I drank again? Would everything be a complete waste if I had to start back at day one? Would Recovery Elevator be a failure? Would I be a failure? Absolutely not, but when we start defining success on clock time, while ignoring the current internal emotional state, then we've missed the mark. The truth is that most people reset their sobriety tracker multiple times. In 2014 alone, I had countless day ones. Again, recovery is not black or white and success in sobriety is much more than a ticking clock.

Be careful with statements like, "When I have one year of sobriety, then I'll be okay," or "At two years of sobriety, things will fall into place." Although it's true things begin to smooth out the longer we go without drinking, be aware of tying happiness or an outcome to a future date because that removes the possibility of being happy in this moment.

Stop saying ONLY. One of the biggest pet peeves of mine is when I hear someone say, "I *only* have three days of sobriety," or "It's *only* been 65 days since my last drink." It hurts my heart when I see people feel insufficient because they don't have a certain amount of days without a drink. The only gauge of success is the fact that you've embarked on this courageous journey. Everything else is minor details. You've decided to turn the gaze inward and that takes courage! If you logged three days last month without a drink, then go buy yourself a scone. Nice job! If 75% of days in 2018 were alcohol free, then throw a party and be sure to invite me!

As Siddhartha Gautama, the Buddha, would say, the root of all suffering is attachment, and be careful you don't attach your self-worth and identity to a sobriety tracker. If you've been to 12 Step meetings, you'll notice it's the same person who always lets you know how long they've been sober. Sure, some of us may be further along this journey but we are all equal. To prove this point, I've seriously considered making a YouTube video on my five-year AF anniversary where I take a sip of beer, purposefully putting me back at day one. My self-worth has nothing to do with a clock and yours doesn't either.

It's important to keep in mind what we're really tracking. If the tracker says we've gone 453 days without a drink, but we can't stop eating sugar, started smoking again and the thinking mind is torturing us, we may have only been tracking the amount of time that the *why* behind the drinking hasn't been addressed.

I'm a firm believer that full abstinence from alcohol is where we'll end up, but this isn't where most people start. Once the heart and soul have been merged, you'll be tracking way cooler shit, like how many countries you've been to, or how many half marathons you've run. Don't place too much emphasis on tracking how long you've been avoiding something, but focus on how many times you've meditated, or hiked to your favorite viewpoint to watch the sunset.

Saddle up

☐ Have you found yourself attaching success or self-worth to a future sobriety date?

☐ Are you able to feel successful regardless of how much time away from alcohol you have?

☐ Have you ever said, "I *only* have _____ amount of days?"

☐ What are some other things you'd like to track on this journey?

You Are Doing This

I remember waking up one morning in July 2014 with a pounding headache, filled with shame because I drank, again, the night before despite promising myself that I wouldn't, and I started off the morning with the familiar pep talk of, "I can do this." While repeating this phrase, I interrupted myself and said, "wait a second, this isn't a matter of I can do this, *I am doing this*." We've all heard the saying that half the battle is showing up and what I didn't recognize that morning was that I had been showing up the past four years. Even though logging consecutive days without a drink wasn't a strong skillset of mine at the time, I was still doing it. When we resolutely announce, "I can do this," at the unconscious level, we send ourselves a message that at some later date something of importance will be achieved, and the infinite power of the present moment is then stripped away. No matter where you are on this journey, don't forget you are doing this and you're doing an incredible job, despite what the thinking brain might be saying.

Saddle up

☐ Tell yourself, I am already doing this. Own it.

☐ Remind yourself that progress is always being made, regardless of where you are on the journey.

Healing Symptoms

These are the more commonly called 'post-acute withdrawal symptoms/syndrome' (PAWS) which is the body reaching a new mental homeostasis after the initial physical withdrawal process has finished. Even though some medical professionals will use the word syndrome, don't worry, nothing is malfunctioning. In fact, throw out the word syndrome. This period can last anywhere from three to nine months depending on the individual and although this can be uncomfortable at times, it's important to welcome these peaks and valleys in emotional and physical states as signs that the body is healing, because that's exactly what is happening. The are several systems in your body that are reaching a new equilibrium without alcohol and this takes time. Sometimes the body will undershoot or overshoot the chemical mark, and this can be difficult to tolerate but keep in mind, just as the body knows how to heal a broken bone, it knows exactly what it's doing; let it happen.

It's understandable to wake up one day in sobriety and say, "Fuck, I feel like shit, there has to be something wrong with me," and upon visiting a doctor they will do their best to find something wrong with you and possibly put you on a medication to blunt or numb the very emotions that need to be felt. Again, there is nothing wrong with you and I encourage you to fully embrace these emotional tornadoes as friendly reminders that you're on the right track.

Most likely alcohol has been used to mask feelings of unworthiness or past traumas and the resurfacing of these emotions will be intense at times. These suppressed energetic systems and emotions need to be expressed and it's all part of the healing process. If it's been six months without a drink and a certain emotional state persists, the body is pointing where to go next on this journey. These healing symptoms can be the best of teachers if we are open to listening. As spiritual thought leader Thich Nhat Hanh says, "When we give ourselves the chance to let go of all our tension, the body's natural capacity to heal itself can begin to work." I have a YouTube video where I talk more in depth about these healing symptoms (PAWS) if you'd like to learn more.

Saddle up

☐ Have you experienced intense emotional and physical swings in early sobriety? What were they?

☐ Remind yourself that these uncomfortable emotions are healthy and that it's all part of the healing process.

☐ Do you trust that your body has the full capacity to heal itself physically and mentally?

☐ Allow yourself to heal.

Surrender

This is perhaps the most nebulous concept in recovery since, according to 12 Step programs, it suggests we must fully give up control, admit that we are powerless over alcohol, and accept help from a higher power before we can successfully depart from alcohol. Yikes, that's a lot to unpack and I'd like to simplify this important concept. Sure it's true that while after interviewing over 250 people on the podcast nearly all, including myself, reached a moment of surrender, but I don't feel it's a requirement we let go of the reins of life, roll over in submission to alcohol and invite God into the driver's seat of life. Surrender is simply yielding to the next stage or chapter in life. As I previously mention, addictions are no more than signposts and surrender is when we fully accept them as teachers and are ready to make what will most likely be the most important change in our life: quitting alcohol. As the 13th century Sufi poet Rumi says, "The moment you accept what troubles you've been given, the door will open."

This moment of surrender, which one would practically assume encompasses feelings of defeat and utter failure, is actually liberating and empowering. Internally, we stop trying to control everything. Once we reach a moment when we realize there are no more ways to "moderate" in the playbook, and we can clearly see that controlled drinking constantly results in a dumpster fire, we usually find ourselves saying, "Fuck, I quit," or "I'm done," or "I can't do this anymore." If you've ever muttered those words or something similar, congratulations, you've hit what I like to call the "now what?" milestone, which is huge because it means you've mentally stopped projecting a future that involves alcohol in it. This is when the extremely important memo of "I'm done drinking," makes it past the analytical part of the brain to the subconscious, and shortly after that enters the proverbial "moment of clarity." Our next step of action comes from intuition and not the thinking mind, and we reach out to a friend or colleague who doesn't drink, we enter "quit drinking podcast" in the iTunes search bar, or go to an A.A. meeting, to name a few.

If you're wondering if you've had a moment of surrender or not, most likely you've had several mini-surrender moments which led you to reading this book. Don't worry, just like rock bottom moments, if we ignore or miss them, these opportunities to fully yield to the next chapter of life will continually present themselves until we have to listen. Surrendering can be difficult, especially for overly competitive people, since it means we stop fighting. We are constantly told to get back up in life when knocked down, which is applicable to nearly every other problem in life, but not when it comes to alcohol. The moment we surrender, accept what is, life can then unfold and the magic will start to happen.

My most intense moment of surrender came on Friday night, August 29th, 2014 when I was DJing a wedding in Big Sky, Montana. While setting up, and during cocktail hour, I made frequent trips to the open bar and with roughly five hours left in the wedding, I found myself drunk. I remember standing behind the DJ table, with some sappy country love song playing, and knew at the gut level I was done fighting and needed help. The universe was also on board with this plan. I was the owner of a DJ business at the time and another DJ of mine had just finished a fundraiser event only three miles away and he arrived to finish the wedding. I then called a friend, told her exactly what was going on, and she drove 45 miles and picked me up. On the way back to Bozeman, I repeatedly called my mom, dad, and brother, to tell them I was ready to seek treatment, go to rehab, but none of them picked up. The next day, when my dad called me back and asked me what's wrong, I said "Hey Dad, I was calling to let you know I need treatment, to go to rehab, but give me a day or two. I think I can do this." That Saturday morning on August 30th, I woke up feeling different because I had reached the "now what?" milestone and started working *with* life energy as opposed to against it. My last drink on came on September 6th, 2014 when I was on a camping trip with friends. I drank 1/2 a beer, poured the rest out, got in my car and drove back home. It wasn't fun telling people why I was leaving, but my body knew that we were done going against the flow of life.

Saddle up

☐ What does surrender mean to you?

☐ Ask yourself if you've surrendered to the next chapter in your life? If not, what do you think is holding you back?

☐ Do you think strength is found in surrender?

☐ Write down any moments of surrender you've experienced.

☐ Do you think surrender is necessary in order to quit drinking?

The Pink Cloud

When the body and mind are no longer processing copious amounts of the drug called alcohol, you're physically going to start feeling better and should experience enhanced mental clarity as well. Systems in the body, which have been on overload for quite some time, get a much-needed break resulting in a reduction of inflammation and an overall sense of wellbeing throughout the body. For most, the euphoric pink cloud shows up around months 1-2 and lingers for another 6-12 months. If you don't experience the pink cloud in early sobriety, congratulations, you get a head start in this journey of introspection and will avoid the "coming back to earth" when the pink cloud dissipates. For another group, the pink cloud is here to stay and is the new way of life. There is no right or wrong way to do this.

When it's raining outside, it's too late to fix the roof. If and when the pink cloud does arrive, this is the time to push the boundaries of the comfort zone and add as much as you possibly can to your recovery portfolio because this period of clarity may soon pass, and life can happen at any moment. It was during the pink cloud, in my first ten months AF, that I had the energy and mental coherence to build Recovery Elevator, which I'm a firm believer has saved my life.

Saddle up

- ☐ Have you experienced the pink cloud?
- ☐ What physical benefits have you seen without alcohol in your life?
- ☐ What do you think the pink cloud is?
- ☐ Remind yourself that during the pink cloud is the time to focus on you.

Relapse

For some, and I've only met a few, relapse isn't part of their story, but it is for the vast majority and it is nothing to be ashamed about. Some people make the decision to quit drinking and never look back. I made the decision to quit drinking 1,000 times and looked back 999 times. I feel relapse is another word that needs to be thrown out because of its implications of failure, "all is lost" and a need to start over. Phrases such as "slip up," "off the wagon" and "whoopsie daisy" also need to be set aside because they don't accurately describe what's really taking place. When we drink again, we are simply doing additional "field research" or "navel gazing" and learning necessary lessons along the way. I personally needed to conduct volumes of field research (I had hundreds of day ones), to learn the invaluable lessons that have built the foundations of my sobriety today.

If you do find yourself in an intense period of "field research," self-compassion is key, and do your best to recognize that this is all part of the process. You may feel you've done enough research for you and your entire book club, but keep in mind that the unconscious mind is usually sitting in the back of the classroom paying little attention. You may be periodically doing field research while reading this book which is completely fine. Simply said, relapse isn't a big deal. Stop placing success and failure parameters on if you drank last night or not. I'm a firm believer that if we start addressing what we're using alcohol to cover up, then relapse, aka field research will become less frequent and even a thing of the past. That is where efforts need to be focused.

When you do find yourself on stable footing, or in uncharted waters, beware of the three most dangerous words on this journey, "I got this." If your inner dialogue says something like, "We just went 30 days without a drink, I got this!" try to observe where this voice is coming from. If it's from the gut or intuition, then maybe you're on a sturdy foundation, but it usually comes from the thinking mind. In my experience, every time I said, "Fuck yeah, I got this," I found myself in a period of intense field research followed by a, "What the fuck just happened?" Confidence is great, but it is important we recognize which inner voice is talking.

If I do relapse, I would embrace it as an opportunity to internally explore what parts of the personality are in need of healing. If I had just one wish in life, I'd wish to never drink again, but I've also been doing this long enough to realize the need for additional field research can take place at any time and can happen to anyone. However, if I focus more on the inner currency of peace, and less on "not drinking" the need for additional field research should dissolve.

Saddle up

- ☐ Has relapse or field research been part of your story?
- ☐ What do you think of relapse? Do you view it as a failure or an opportunity?
- ☐ After conducting field research, are you able to see trends emerging?
- ☐ If you do find yourself on day one, write down why you think you drank. What were you feeling at the time? Where were you, who were you with?
- ☐ Compassionately tell yourself you deserve this, regardless of how much field research you've been conducting.
- ☐ What are your thoughts on the three most dangerous words "I got this?"

Chapter 10
Get Off the Elevator

"You might need to ditch the booze if...family members always make a point of saying "we restocked our liquor cabinet for you" when you're coming to visit."

—Chris, Oregon

This is the most exciting part of the book because you start to build the foundation for a new life without alcohol. Quitting drinking doesn't have to suck, in fact, it can be a lot of fun. Tell yourself, "This is going to be fun." The real creative you will begin to emerge and the unification of the heart and soul will be beautiful. As the interviewee Jeff says in Episode 203 of the Recovery Elevator podcast, "Look at this time in your life as an experiment of sorts." I encourage you to try as many of these techniques and strategies as possible but not all at once. Some strategies may be beneficial in early sobriety and others will play a more important role further down the road. This chapter is a culmination of the strategies I have personally implemented as well as others I have learned from interviews on the podcast and in-person conversations with those who have been successful in ditching the booze.

As Lily Tomlin says, "For fast-acting relief, try slowing down." Most of us want to load the sobriety toolkit the instant we decide alcohol is no longer serving us, but I don't recommend this. Don't forget, the entanglement with alcohol took place over years, perhaps decades, and the disentanglement process may follow a similar timeline. Again, when taking this journey slow, I encourage you to cut back on multitasking because we want to take actions with mindfulness and presence. Implement these strategies at a pace much more slowly than you feel necessary in order not to miss the subtle cues which all point toward happiness in life. If we hastily check the boxes in recovery, as if it's a destination of sorts, we are prone to miss the myriad of signposts showing us where to go next on this journey. When going too fast, we miss the blooming flower, the dogs playing in the park, the cascade of colors in the sky, and Third Eye Blind playing in the background at your favorite coffee shop. Is there too slow of a pace? Well, as Confucius said, "It doesn't matter how slow you go, as long as you don't stop."

It's important to keep in mind that all improvement and growth on this journey will be preceded by letting go of something. Space in your life needs to be created first before abundance, happiness and joy can enter. The ego nearly always throws a mini-fit before and after each burst of personal growth and you'll start to become aware of this process and even welcome the uncomfortable feelings. At first, you'll find it convenient to place narratives on the uncomfortable emotions, but within time, you'll recognize these anchorings as simply the removal of inner gunk as your foundation becomes sturdier. It's important to let this purge of unhealthy thoughts, relationships, and behaviors unfold as it's intended because it's going to happen regardless. The first and most obvious thing to go will be the alcohol, but shortly after, in order of importance: the people, places, ideas, thought patterns and behaviors that are no longer in line with your new life direction will leave, if you allow them to. It's of paramount importance to recognize what is happening and embrace it. You may find that a dear friend, or a group of friends, congratulate you on your decision to quit drinking, and then find them drift away. Remember, this decluttering will be followed by healthier altruistic relationships, more inner peace and an abundance of joy.

As you implement these strategies, it's important to focus on the action and not the results. You're entering a new chapter in life, the unknown, where anything is possible and having a predetermined outcome can lead to self-sabotage. Do not attach yourself to a specific outcome. You cannot control results, only the action. As the ancient Sanskrit scripture, the *Bhahavad Gita* says, "You have a right to your actions, but never to the results of your actions. Act for the actions' sake." Okay, let's get started.

Burn the Ships > Accountability > Community

In 1519, Hernán Cortés landed in Veracruz, Mexico with 500 soldiers, 100 sailors, and 16 horses to begin his great conquest to take over the Aztec Empire, which at the time was one of the world's richest empires. This vast wealth had been held by the Aztecs for over 600 years. Everybody knew this because army after army, conqueror after conqueror had tried to seize this wealth and power, but nobody had been able to do it. Upon arriving after the long voyage, Cortés gathered the men up on the beach and said three words, "Burn the ships." I imagine he dropped his sword, which is the modern-day equivalent of a mic drop and walked off the beach. Since retreat was no longer an option with the burning of the ships, Hernán Cortés was able to capture the Aztec empire.

I didn't find traction on this journey until I started to burn the ships and let others know about my goal of quitting drinking. Let's pump the brakes for a second as I know the thought of opening up to others about our drinking causes anxiety levels to spike; we're gonna burn the ships at a slow pace…but it needs to happen. This, by far, was the most important thing I did on my journey. I first got honest with myself, then my mom, dad, brother, my fantasy football league (Sean, Brady, Pete, TJ, Paul E., Jesse—thanks for being so supportive, guys), doctors, physicians, psychologist, employers (yes, I did say employers), neighbors and eventually on social media. These weren't casual in-passing statements but sit-down conversations which I like to call "reverse interventions." I had clear, detailed, conversations about what my drinking looked like, the emotional pain it has caused and how I need their help and support. I also apologized for the burden my drinking placed on the relationship. When having a reverse intervention don't dance around the subject. Be direct, thorough and get to the point.

I wasn't able to take back these conversations. I wasn't able to walk up to my neighbor Rick and say, "Hey Rick, remember last week when

I told you I was buzzed 90% of February, and how I have solo drinking expeditions at home most nights and when I empty the bottles in the trash I first check to make sure you're not outside doing yardwork? Yeah, I was just joking." I couldn't un-say those things. I had my first official burning of the ships conversation in May of 2014. I had been covertly drinking alone since 5:30 a.m. on a houseboat in Lake Powell in southern Utah and at 7:30 a.m., I walked into my parents' room, woke them up and said, "I gotta tell you two something." Later that day, I had a similar one-on-one conversation with my brother. It's no coincidence my sobriety date was a few months later.

If you're feeling uneasy about this, I understand. When I uploaded the first episode of the Recovery Elevator podcast to iTunes that basically announced, "Hello, Planet Earth, I have a drinking problem," I remember saying to myself, "Oh fuck, what have I done?" I laid awake at night for three months after the first episode came out mumbling, "oh shit, what did I do?" No joke. And what happens when we talk about it? Read this next part carefully because this is where it gets neat and may surprise you. I've heard countless stories of people telling others, posting their stories on Facebook, creating blogs, podcasts and I've yet to hear one bad outcome and this mirrors my personal experience. When I hit one year of sobriety, I was terrified of making a public Facebook post about my struggles with alcohol, but I knew I had to do it. The post had over 500 likes, over 150 supportive comments and I received another 20 private messages of encouragement from others who were questioning their drinking. This post, by a long shot, garnered more interaction on social media than any other one, and it was ALL positive and supportive. Just three years after the first episode launched on iTunes, I found myself surrounded by a kickass group of people who don't drink, in a new career, experiencing inner peace for days, and touring Machu Picchu with twenty other sober badasses. How cool is that! There is no way to tell for certain, but if I didn't burn the ships, I don't think I'd be on this planet anymore.

The best way to burn the ships, or have these reverse interventions is to have scheduled, sit-down, one-on-one conversations with people who are closest to you. Let them know this isn't a diet or fad, and you'll need their support. Perhaps let them in on some of your rock bottom moments and you may need to make an apology (or fifty) for something you did while drinking.

When you do burn the ships, here are the four main responses you'll get, and it's important to keep in mind that their reactions have absolutely, unequivocally, nothing to do with you.

1. "Hell yeah, that's awesome."—Their response will be supportive and almost underwhelming because despite how special you think you are (I was the same way), people don't notice or care if you're drinking or not.

2. "No way, my brother [mother, sister, cousin, neighbor, friend…] is also struggling with addiction."—Remember there are over 20 million Americans struggling with an alcohol use disorder. Nearly everyone knows someone who is going toe-to-toe with alcohol.

3. "Really? How much did you drink?"—When people start inquiring about how much you drank, they are usually questioning their own drinking. You'll get this response about 10% of the time.

4. "Good luck with that."—Despite thinking this will be the common response, it's extremely rare, and in fact, I've yet to encounter it face to face. Keep in mind, people who aren't supportive of your new badass self (not drinking will be the most badass thing about you) will either come around or drift away.

The reason I led off with burning the ships as the first action item is because it inevitably opens the door to the next two most important components: accountability and community. The primary purpose of the podcast was to create accountability and it worked. I didn't care who listened, as long as I remained AF. As the number of individuals holding me accountable increased, a community was being built without my knowing it. Looking back, launching a podcast at six months alcohol-free was risky, but it paid off.

I remember being in a bar with some friends around 6 months AF when a bartender approached me and asked if I wanted a soda. Since bartenders don't usually walk out from behind the bar, over to where you're standing and offer you a drink, she could see my confusion and she said, "I listen to your podcast and if I see you with a drink in your hand, I'll kick you in the nuts." How cool is that? Not the kick in the nuts part, but the decision to burn the ships had created accountability that I could never have predicted.

I used to own an arcade business and around one-year AF, I found myself in a bar around lunch time speaking with the owner about the possibility of placing arcade games in the bar. After our conversation, I turn around and see a friendly face I recognize. He asked me how I was doing. I could tell there was more weight behind his question than the normal "hey, how's it going." He then proceeded to tell me that he saw my vehicle in the parking lot of a bar and wanted to check in to make sure I wasn't getting canned. I didn't know this guy well, yet he was there to help me remain AF. What if I was there to drink? This guy may have prevented it. The decision to come out about my struggles with alcohol created accountability in all parts of my life.

This accountability eventually blossomed into a community that gives me back ten times what I put into it. There were definitely some growing pains as Recovery Elevator turned into a business but now the community (Cafe RE) is my tribe and I want to thank everyone who helped build it. Seriously, I want to take a moment to thank everyone who has signed up for Café RE. Without your support and inspiration, this book doesn't happen. You all have been the best of teachers and I will never forget the lessons each and every one of you has taught me. You all FILL my heart.

Community is the main driver of my happiness today. The Harvard happiness study (also known as the Harvard Study of Adult Development), which is the longest running study ever performed on happiness, has proved that embracing community helps us live longer and be happier. Scientists began tracking the health of 268 Harvard sophomores during the Great Depression in 1938 in hopes that a longitudinal study would reveal clues to leading healthy and happy lives. Of the original Harvard cohort recruited as part of the Grant Study, only 19 are still alive, all in their mid-90s. Among the original recruits were eventual President John F. Kennedy and longtime Washington Post editor Ben Bradlee. What they found was that close relationships, more than money or fame, are what keep people happy throughout their lives. Close ties to community are what enable humans to feel part of something bigger than themselves. Those bonds protect people from life's discontents, help to delay mental and physical decline, and are better predictors of long and happy lives than social class, IQ, or even genes. In addition, several studies found that people's level of satisfaction with their relationships at age 50 was a better predictor of physical health than their cholesterol levels were.

If you're wondering how in the hell you're going to build this supportive community, again, I encourage you to focus on the action and not the results. The universe also wants you to become AF and when you embark on this journey, the right people will be ushered into your life. At around one year AF, a close friend of mine named Dusty (Episode 206) quit drinking right when I desperately needed sober companionship and over the past couple of years, we have had so much fun together without a single drop of booze.

The best way to create accountability, which inevitably leads to community, is to build it one conversation at a time. This can be done online in a sober community and then ideally in person. There is no need to overthink this process and please don't do it out of fear. Set fire to the ships, not out of fear that you'll end up drunk in a ditch, but trusting a better, more authentic life awaits. I want you to have these important one-on-one conversations because you know a happier life is right around the corner and not out of the fear that you'll end up drunk and ruining your cousin Mike's wedding. It's important to create accountability not only with sober people but with normal drinkers as well. Today, with the internet, it's never been easier to create accountability with access to online sober communities.

In 2010, I was wondering how in the hell I was going to stay sober at an upcoming bachelor party in Las Vegas. I knew there was little chance of me making it through AF unless I let someone in on my goal not to drink so I got outside my comfort zone and emailed my college roommate Spencer who was also attending the event. It took me probably two hours to compose the three-line email and another 30 minutes hovering around the send button before I finally sent it. I was terrified to open his reply, but when I did, it went something like this. "Hey dude, that's awesome. I'll be sure to drink block all drinks headed your way, just like you cockblocked all the chicks for me in college." With Spencer's help, I made it through the bachelor party and the wedding a couple of months later sober. If you're worried about an upcoming social event, I highly recommend sending an email or text to someone who will also be in attendance letting them know you won't be drinking. They want to help.

Another reason why burning the ships is so important is because you have the power to save a life. You never know who is hanging on by a thread and your courage to come forward as someone who no longer drinks may be the catalyst for change in their life. The decision to open up about your new life direction will overlap into the lives of others and the ripples will last for eternity.

Saddle up

- ☐ Visualize burning the ships. Take note of the emotions you feel before and after. Do you feel lighter after visually telling someone about your goal to quit drinking?

- ☐ Write down the people who know about your struggles with alcohol or your goal to quit drinking. Then write five more down and create a plan to inform them. Be as clear as you can with them and don't beat around the bush.

- ☐ What are the reactions you've experienced when you've burned the ships? Were they supportive? Did they surprise you? Have you experienced a negative reaction? If so, it's important to recognize this has nothing to do with you.

- ☐ Have you noticed people, places, things ideas have exited your life now that you no longer wish to have alcohol in your life? Have you fought this process?

- ☐ If you have an upcoming social event on your calendar such as a wedding, birthday party, or anniversary, reach out to someone who will be attending and create accountability before the event.

- ☐ Write down who consists of your AF community. Make it a goal to add 1-2 people per month. Don't forget to include normal drinkers. Make it a point to connect in person daily, weekly and monthly.

Emotions

Before the age of five, most of us are taught we shouldn't have uncomfortable feelings, and heaven forbid we express them. In addition, human beings have an exceptional ability to fix onto what life is supposed to look like and how we're supposed to feel. After scrolling Facebook or Instagram for an hour, it's difficult not to feel like something is wrong with you...remember, there is nothing wrong with you. This next idea is important: emotions, all of them, are your ally and are always working in your favor. Do not deny or ignore them because this is never sustainable in the long run. The healthiest thing you can do is admit and become aware of an uncomfortable emotion because avoiding them inevitably results in a full eruption at a later date.

Don't label emotions as positive/negative or good/bad. In fact, this may sound strange, but humans aren't very good at knowing whether an emotion is healthy or unhealthy. We attach an incorrect label to an energetic pattern and often "double down" on an emotion and find ourselves being mad that we're mad, or anxious about being anxious. Like weather passing through the sky, let emotions come and go without a desire for a different inner state.

All emotions need to be expressed and if you want a good example of how to do this, watch a toddler. A baby doesn't let emotions build but releases the energy as it arises. They can go from a complete emotional dump to laughing hysterically a few minutes later. Unfortunately, at an early age, we are taught to stifle this healthy behavior which leads to a bottleneck of unprocessed emotions which for me exploded on February 4th, 2018 with nearly three and a half years AF. I woke up that morning with an intense emotional charge that had been building for years and I could no longer ignore it. What happened next was a level 10 meltdown, which is an incorrect label since it was the best thing that could have happened.

It was a melt in, or a melt up. During this inner melding of sorts, the unconscious was on a manhunt for the soul and I started to release energy by smacking my chest. This evolved into me yelling at the top of my lungs in my closet while hitting the side of my head with open palms. There was such an excess of energy needing to be released, that I found myself on the floor with two black eyes, and I felt completely liberated. For probably the first time since I was a kid, I gave the body permission to release this tightly compacted stored energy. It wasn't pretty by any means, but afterwards, it felt so good. My body knew exactly what it was doing and the violent expression of these caged-up emotional charges is exactly what needed to happen. Nowadays, I have developed healthier ways than a personal sparring match to release this excess energy and no longer let it build up. If sitting in a particularly uncomfortable energetic pattern becomes too intense, I might yell into a blanket, hit a pillow with a tennis racket, or hike into a forest and scream as loud as I can. Not because anything in particular is wrong, but the body has indicated there is an excess of energy that needs to be released. Below are some additional ways I use to ground myself in periods of intense emotional charge:

- I walk outside barefooted. This is called grounding or earthing. You, all people, animals, plants, and inanimate objects are electrical beings living in an electrical world. Everything that's made of atoms (everything) has a net charge that's either positive, negative, or neutral. Grounding means discharging built-up static electricity directly into the earth. The earth has a negative charge, and you have a positive charge. This is why walking barefooted on the beach or in grass feels so damn good!
- I acknowledge what is happening. Anxiety is great at tricking you into believing that something is real. So, all these fear-based thoughts you are having are simply that: thoughts. Once this is recognized, all I do is wait out the energetic charge.
- You are nature, and so am I. When I'm feeling unease, I try to get out into nature. Ideally, pick a location with a soundtrack such as a stream, birds chirping, or the sound of the wind in the trees and take your shoes off if possible. Simply "be" in the most natural restorative setting.

- I think in terms of "we." Which of these two sentences sounds better? 1. I am struggling right now. 2. We are struggling right now. Most of us orient our thoughts to the individual self, but science is showing that we receive a great benefit when we think of terms of "we," which isn't a lie because we are all connected. It's totally fine to struggle on this journey, but there is no need to struggle alone.

- When I'm not feeling grounded, I start paying close attention to where the discomfort resides in the body, and for me, it's usually in the stomach and solar plexus area. When I place my awareness in this area, I realize my stomach muscles are tight and my breaths are shallow.

- I reach out to a friend. You might be wondering why this isn't on the top of the list, and that's because this is an external action to mitigate inner turmoil. If you do reach out to someone, be careful not to place too much weight on their labeling of your emotions.

Saddle up

☐ What do you do when you feel an uncomfortable emotion? Do you notice the mind labeling it as good or bad?

☐ When was the last time you added more negative energy to an emotion? Have you been sad that you're sad? Angry about being angry? Or resenting a person even more for resenting them in the first place?

☐ Are you in tune with the body when it needs to release excess energy? How do you release this energy? Try smacking a pillow or yelling as loud as you can in your closet.

☐ How do you ground yourself when you experience uncomfortable emotions?

☐ Take your shoes off and walk in nature. Notice how the body feels— your feet, your skin, the empty spaces inside your body.

☐ Tell yourself "we" are going to be fine. Tell yourself, "we" are fine.

Love yourself and lighten up

With absolutely no exception, and your life depends on this, love yourself and never take yourself too seriously. I've yet to meet someone who has been successful on this AF journey who didn't address the issue of self-loathing. Despite what the mind has been telling you for probably quite some time, the universe doesn't expect you to be the next Buddha. It simply wants you to recognize what the soul has known all along, which is that you're perfect just the way you are. Seriously, deep down, inside your core being, you know that nothing was missed upon your creation, and there is a vast reservoir of love that desperately wants to be reunited with you—again. The inner child, which stays the same age for eternity, knows the limitations of external pursuits in life and that nothing in life is that big of a deal. Nothing. The main goal in life isn't to climb some silly corporate ladder, buy a big house, follow the keto diet to perfection, or stockpile a shit ton of money in a bank account. Your true inner self knows these endeavors don't lead to happiness and it wants you to buy a puppy, take a spontaneous road trip to Glacier National Park, take a pottery class, learn how to play "Somewhere Over the Rainbow" on the ukulele and find your tribe. It took me a while to fully grasp this as well, but we're supposed to be happy regardless of how much "stuff" we have or "success" we experience in life. This was perhaps the biggest lesson that my royal rumble with alcohol has taught me. An action item I highly recommend that you do, is change the background photo on your phone to your favorite baby picture of yourself. Every time I look at my phone, I see an angelic blond-haired kid who just walked two miles with a cricket on his hand. I love that five-year-old kid so much. That kid is still me and he knows that laughter and love are WAY more important in life than podcast download stats and equity in houses.

I want you to love yourself, unconditionally, throughout every part of this journey. It doesn't matter if you've made the decision to quit drinking 500 times and come up short 500 times, love yourself and accept the infinite abundance of love that is omnipresent at all times. Give yourself permission to receive this universal love. It's okay. You deserve it. I know you deserve it. At first, and this might sound strange, it may be uncomfortable not to repeatedly beat yourself up over every mistake you make. If you drink again, I want you to tell yourself, "Who cares, this isn't that big of a deal and I'm doing my best." I want you to repeat that line, or something similar to it while looking at yourself six inches from a mirror. Stare into your eyes and repeat a mantra of self-worth for five minutes. Something neat starts to happen. You'll start communicating with the soul.

Humor is your best vitamin in recovery. Hands down. This is why I've started each chapter off with a "you might have a drinking problem if" line. Do your best to find ways to laugh, smile and to generate laughter in other people's lives as well. Again, recovering who we were always meant to be can be a lot of fun. Have a YouTube session where you watch hilarious cat and dog videos, go to stand-up comedy shows, binge-watch your favorite comedies, do some Mad Libs, and put a smile on your face. In fact, until the smiles come naturally, put a fake smile on your face. Studies show the body doesn't know the difference between a fake and real smile anyways. Part of this journey is trying out fun new hobbies. Now is the time to dabble in whittling, restoring furniture, origami, watercolor painting, underwater photography, archery on horseback or join a roller-skating gang! Now is the time to listen to what your body, not the mind, has been yearning to do all along.

Keep in mind that the only person who has made "not drinking" into a big deal is yourself. Please don't take offense at this, but you're not nearly special enough for everyone on the planet to stop what they're doing and say "Whoa, Susan isn't drinking at a baby shower," or "Joel is having a Diet Coke at happy hour? WTF?" Nobody cares. The host of a party isn't floating around making sure everyone is drinking. None of these scenarios we conjure up are real. The spotlight isn't on you 24/7, despite what the thinking mind wants us to believe and this should come as a relief.

In the process of writing this book, I've had to remind myself to lighten up and realize this is just a book. This book might be good, it might be bad, it might be a complete pile of mediocrity; in the end, it doesn't really matter as long as I do my best and enjoy myself along the way. For that reason, I'm going to insert a joke. What did 0 say to 8? Nice belt.

Saddle up

☐ Change the wallpaper on your phone to your favorite photo of yourself as a kid. PLEASE DO THIS. Every time you unlock your phone, say "I love you," to that kid.

☐ What is something your heart has always wanted to do? If you could travel anywhere in the world, where would it be? Write this down. And then write three things that are holding you back.

☐ What are some new hobbies or activities you want to try? Write them down and try one.

☐ If you find yourself on day 1, tell yourself it's not a big deal and that you love yourself regardless of where you're at in life.

Sobriety Muscles-Coping Skills

Each time you make it through a craving, social event, wedding, party, or the second half of Nicolas Cage's movies without taking a drink, you're building sobriety muscles. When we make it past a situation that normally would involve alcohol, we create new neural connections in the brain, build new circuits in the body and start developing a new set of healthier habits and routines which become the new norm. As we build these sobriety muscles, we start developing coping skills that don't involve alcohol. Prior to quitting drinking, I had four coping mechanisms: Bud Light Tall Boys, Jose Cuervo, Grey Goose and box wine. Keep in mind, simply making it through an event AF, no matter how uncomfortable it can be, is a huge win, because you're departing from old habits.

As you build these coping mechanisms, which are mentioned throughout this book, keep in mind not to come out of the gates at a full sprint. For example, if you're recently AF and you've got an upcoming party, you probably don't need to be the last guest to leave and be sure to always have an exit strategy that isn't dependent on someone else. Don't offer to be the designated driver, especially in early sobriety, because you may find yourself trapped, surrounded by a bunch of drunken goons. Drunk people can be a source of the purest sobriety fuel as you watch them incoherently speak, stumble around, and derail their social lives, but it's important to keep your distance at first. I interviewed a guy on the podcast whose plan to make it through social events, since it was a big part of his job, was to purposefully place himself in these environments for set periods of time. For example, the first week, he went to a restaurant where he sat at the bar for fifteen minutes, then thirty minutes the next week, and so forth. He practiced ordering AF drinks with conviction and started to rewrite his future in these settings.

It's important to start building healthy routines early in an AF life. After reading Hal Elrod's *Miracle Morning*, I woke up at 5:15 a.m. for the first couple years away from booze and during the first hour of each day I journaled, meditated, exercised, did something creative, read a self-help book and practiced positive affirmations. I'll admit, waking up that early was rough for the first month, but then that first hour became the most enjoyable hour of the day. A habit is something you so much that your body knows how to do it better than the mind. This is why when drinking, a drink seemed to magically appear in my hand. Now is the time to start building those healthier habits that will pay major dividends for the remainder of your life.

Saddle up

☐ What new coping skills are you hoping to implement?

☐ Have you made it through a social event AF? How did it feel before, during and after?

☐ Write down three exit strategies you can use if you find yourself uneasy in a social situation and wanting a drink. Remind yourself it's ok to put your well-being first and leave.

☐ What is a new healthy routine you'd like to explore? What does it take to start it?

Plant Medicine

Plant medicines such as psilocybin (magic mushrooms), cannabis (strands with and without THC), ayahuasca, and Ibogaine to name a few, already do and will play a larger role in addiction treatment. According to professor Matthew Johnson at The John Hopkins School of Medicine, these plant medicines can be used to change all sorts of behaviors, not just addiction. The key, in his view, is their power to occasion a sufficiently dramatic experience to "slap people out of their story." It's literally a reboot of the system—a biological control-alt-delete. Plant medicine has the capacity to open a window of mental flexibility in which people can let go of the mental models we use to organize reality. Currently, clinical trials with psilocybin are being fast tracked by the FDA and are in the last phase of testing. Most likely, within a few years of the publication of this book, under the supervision of a psychiatrist or other licensed practitioners, psilocybin guided therapy sessions will be administered to treat depression, anxiety, PTSD and addiction.

Most people don't realize that Alcoholics Anonymous might not have happened without plant medicine. Bill W., one of the original two founding members of A.A., credited his own sobriety to a mystical experience he had on Belladonna, a plant-derived alkaloid with hallucinogenic properties that was administered to him at Towns Hospital in Manhattan in 1934. Few members of A.A. know that the whole idea of a spiritual awakening, which he described as seeing a bright white light during this mystical experience in his hospital room, can be traced back to a plant medicine psychedelic trip.

Cannabis is another plant medicine that is beginning to play a larger role in addiction treatment. According to Dr. Michael Steward, the chief medical officer of Denver, Colorado-based cannabis company Endourage, (this is where I get CBD oil) alcohol has been shown to unbalance the body's natural endocannabinoid system by decreasing the number of CB1 receptors in the body and CBD extracts can help put this system back into equilibrium. Dr. Steward also says cannabis has been shown in both human and animal models to be helpful with the alcohol-related issues of irritability, depression, mood swings, liver damage and neuronal damage. These beneficial results can be achieved with CBD dominant strains that won't get the user high. According to Dr. Steward, who has worked with patients in recovery, cannabis is a very safe medication when used appropriately, and it has immense potential to help with AUDs and a variety of other ailments. I want to be clear, the point of this section isn't to give the idea that someone can replace drinking with pot, but to inform readers that non-THC strains can be a beneficial.

According to Michael Pollan in his book, *How to Change Your Brain*, after several decades of suppression and neglect, psychedelics are having a renaissance. A new generation of scientists, many of them inspired by their own personal experience of the compounds, are testing their potential to heal mental illnesses such as depression, anxiety, trauma, and addiction.

The reason why these medicines can have such profound results is that they have the ability to dissolve the ego and give a visceral sense of oneness or connection with the universe. Keep in mind, addiction is an issue of connection and these medicines go right to the source of disconnection. What can be accomplished with years of talk therapy can be achieved in just a few plant medicine sessions.

My journey led me to plant medicine when I attended a week-long ayahuasca retreat at a center in Costa Rica called Rythmia, in April of 2018. When I look back at my life from my deathbed, it will be pre-and post-plant medicine. I know what I'm about to write may discredit this book for some, and that's okay. Plant medicine reached all the way to the root of my internal disconnection because during the months following, the nighttime binge-eating problem I had grappled with for over a decade, my trichotillomania, asthma, the majority of my lower back pain and my self-loathing all disappeared and haven't returned. I used to spend over $100 a month on asthma medication and it's been seven months since I've refilled my Advair prescription. I also haven't taken an antidepressant or ADHD meds since attending Rythmia.

I have always, since a kid, loved snakes, especially rattlesnakes. Despite making countless trips with the sole purpose of finding a rattlesnake, I never found one. On April 10th, 2018, on my birthday, ten minutes before I was going to drink my first cup of ayahuasca, I saw a Rythmia staff member shining a flashlight in a bush nearby. Without thinking, I went outside and asked him what he was looking at and he said it was a rattlesnake that needed to be killed. He gave me, a barefooted guest, the stick, I killed the rattlesnake and then started the next chapter of my life. Plant medicine, somehow, has divine intelligence and it knew that for me to blast through fortified egoic structures in my brain, I was going to need a lot of medicine. On the last night of ceremonies, I drank a hero dose of ayahuasca (7 cups, which I later found out is the record at Rythmia) and howler monkeys showed up to help me out when I found myself in an extremely difficult spot, I kid you not. With my thoughts alone, I was able to control the howls of the howler monkeys, which are the loudest animal on the earth. After confirming with the Shamans and two hotel staff that what I thought was happening was actually happening, my life was forever changed. It was, without a doubt, the most profound moment in my life and it changed me on the molecular and physiological level. For a full recap of my experience, you can listen to episode 170 of the Recovery Elevator podcast, but to summarize, I left with a sense of connection, internal and external, that I'd never felt before and the thought of drinking alcohol, or taking any other harmful substances repulsed me.

Saddle up

☐ Ask yourself if you think plant medicines are acceptable ways to treat addiction? If not, ask yourself why?

Pharmaceutical Meds to help quit drinking

I'm a firm believer that the journey into an AF life can be done without pharmaceutical meds, and I don't have personal experience with these medications, but I feel they do deserve a spot in this book. There are three main medications, with the most popular one being Naltrexone, which blocks brain opioid receptors making drinking less rewarding. The Sinclair Method, which is more popular in Scandinavian countries, consists of taking Naltrexone one hour before drinking. You take a drink, and don't feel the effects. The next medication is Disulfiram/Antabuse which causes the drinker to experience nausea, headaches, excess sweating and vomiting if they drink. Take a drink and you'll feel like ralphing. The third is Campral/Acamprosate, which appears to normalize the alcohol-disrupted brain activity, particularly in the GABA and glutamate neurotransmitter systems. In America, it's reported that these drugs are prescribed less than 2% of the time despite their reported efficacy. The podcast Radiolab has an episode titled "The Fix" where they interview people who have used these medications to curtail their drinking, and although reports show tremendous early progress, in the long run the medications come up short because they don't address the underlying sources of pain that alcohol is being used to cover up. In addition, avoiding alcohol out of fear that a violent reaction will occur when drinking, isn't a sustainable strategy in the long run. What happens if the user decides to skip a night and go out on the town? The majority of people I've spoken with who do have experience with these medications report their end goal is still abstinence, and this has been a useful tool to help them get there.

Saddle up

☐ Have do you feel about these medications? Can a pill cure a drinking problem?

☐ What do you think are the drawbacks to using these medications?

Cravings

In Buddhist philosophy, craving is the root of all suffering. Buddha wasn't talking about Miller Highlife but the desire for an external substance to pacify the inner state. A craving is simply the desire to change the inner state with an external substance or behavior and if you're reading this book, most likely alcohol did the trick. When we first stop drinking, the body is physically craving alcohol but after the initial detoxification process, cravings represent something else: the desire for a different emotional state and it no longer has much to do with alcohol. For example, if you find yourself at thirty days AF and you say, "Damn, I want a drink," it's not the drink you're craving since the body is no longer physically dependent on alcohol, but a desire to depart from the present moment and experience a different emotional state. It's important to recognize this because then we can then start addressing the higher-level question which is, "What discomfort are we using alcohol to cover up?"

A craving is a desire to return to old ways and according to Dr. Joe Dispenza, author of *You Are the Placebo*, cravings are withdrawals from the body's familiar chemical emotional addictions. Dispenza says, "if we can understand our discomfort is simply the biological, neurological, chemical, and even the genetic death of the old self, we have a greater power to change.

I'm not going to bullshit you; cravings can be intense and seem never-ending but it's important not to label these strong emotional charges as bad and to let them pass. Each time we make it through a craving AF, we strengthen the sobriety muscles and gain confidence. Here are some of my favorite strategies to beat cravings.

Cravings have a lifespan and studies show the peaks last an average of twenty minutes. Next time you experience a craving, set a timer on your phone and let it pass. Another strategy is to tell yourself you'll drink after a certain activity. For example, I would to tell myself I could drink after a run. If I still felt like drinking after the run, I would then say, okay, we'll drink after we go get groceries and I'd repeat this process until the emotional charge had passed.

Usually when a craving arrives the mind will start concocting convincing stories such as, "we'll only have one," or "it's going to be different this time." When this happens, do your best to play the tape forward and ask yourself, "What are the chances I'm going to have just one glass of wine, put the cork back in the bottle and fall asleep to Enya?" Most likely, you've got volumes of research behind you indicating there's slim chance that this will be the outcome after taking the first drink.

Physical activities such as going for a run are good, but not ideal since you may be running away from the emotions that need to be felt. Before resorting to physical activity, when a craving arrives, rather than going into your head and trying to figure it out, find a comfortable chair, drop into the body and locate where the craving is located in the body. Once you have pinpointed the location of this surge in energy, breathe into the area, squeeze it with awareness, and let the body know you're there to work with the energy and not against it. According to Dr. Sue Morter, author of *The Energy Codes*, once we do this, the craving will start to melt and infuse itself into the river of consciousness that is trying to birth itself.

Do your best to lean into cravings as much as you can, but if they get too intense, then phone a friend or go for a run. When it comes to working with cravings, it's best to do this solo in order to build sustainable coping skills but reach out the instant you feel the urge to drink too overwhelming.

Saddle up

☐ What do you think cravings are? How do you deal with them? When do you experience them? Can you see patterns with your cravings?

☐ Next time you experience a craving, ask yourself what feeling you'd like to feel that is different than the one you're currently feeling?

☐ Do you think a craving can simply be your body hoping to return to its old routines, thoughts and patterns?

☐ Next time you experience a craving, set a timer for twenty minutes and allow it to pass. Play the tape forward and ask yourself what will actually happen? Will you really have just one drink?

☐ Squeeze where in the body the craving is housed with awareness.

Dating

Removing alcohol in my life simplified many things, especially dating. Now keep in mind, getting dating advice from me is a little like taking stock tips from Bernie Madoff but here's what I've learned so far. It turns out, girls aren't instinctually attracted to guys who prioritize booze over quality conversation and spend weekend mornings in bed with a hangover. When I first started dating in my alcohol-free life, I was hiding the most badass thing about me which was the fact I do "life" without alcohol. I slowly started to realize that this isn't a liability but a killer asset and nowadays I leverage the hell out of it. Most women have had a relationship go south due to alcohol and it's an immediate comfort to them knowing that it won't be an issue. At the unconscious and conscious level, both women and men are looking for a fully present partner who doesn't check out of the relationship with alcohol.

If you're concerned dates will abruptly end after an order for a soda water is placed, I've got good news for you—it's a non-issue. In fact, you've been given the best dating filter one could ask for. I can find out on the first date, usually right after drinks are ordered, if there will be a future or not. If you're anything like me, surface level conversation gets old fast and almost always, without fail, once we start talking about alcohol, we're having conversations that would normally take place at date five or ten and this is refreshing for both parties. There is a worldwide alcohol-free movement taking place and everyone, not just sober people, wants to be part of it. There are dry bars, alcohol free night clubs, and sober music festivals popping up across the globe because people are yearning for an environment where the drug alcohol isn't present. Everyone—including normal drinkers—is starting to wake up and realize that alcohol is what's blocking connection and not what's creating it.

In dating, I highly encourage you to leverage your decision to be AF, because it's something that sets you apart and will work in your favor. If a date asks why you no longer drink, all you need to say is that alcohol no longer fits with the direction you want to go in life. You just became the most interesting date ever. Be proud of the decision to be the best version of you. An AF free life opens the door to countless more exciting options than "dinner and drinks."

Saddle up

☐ Are you nervous to tell a date you don't drink?

☐ What do you think a relationship without alcohol will look like?

☐ Do you think alcohol makes relationships easier or harder?

☐ Visualize and practice telling a date you don't drink and why.

"Would you like a drink?"

When I first quit drinking, I choreographed and rehearsed how I would respond when offered a drink. Looking back, so much brain wattage was wasted on how I would answer that incredibly simple question. Again, since I'm not the focal point of the universe, people don't care if I drink or not and I've yet to hear a record come to a screeching halt after declining an ethanol-filled beverage. The journey into an AF life can be confusing at times, but this one is simple. The absolute best response, hands down, when offered a drink, is "No, thanks," or "I don't drink." There is no need to explain why you're not drinking or get them up to speed on all the emotional pain and turmoil alcohol has caused in your life. 95% of the time, they won't ask why you're not drinking. If they do, ask, they may be asking because they are questioning their own drinking or someone close to them is grappling with alcohol. It's fully up to you to open up or not. You don't owe anyone an explanation about your decision to not drink, but if someone does ask why you're not drinking poison (it's so ironic we have to explain why we're not drinking such a toxic substance), I highly encourage you to use it as an opportunity to create accountability and build community. You might be directly or indirectly helping someone else who is questioning their drinking.

The next time you're offered a drink, I encourage you to skip the story of "I'm on the Atkins diet," "I'm on antibiotics," "I'm training for a 1/2 marathon," and let them know that you simply don't drink. Most likely, you'll have to tell this same person, a month later, that you're still on the Atkins diet, on the meds or still training for a ½ marathon. Save everyone the time, do yourself the favor, and be honest and upfront from the start. It's that simple. Or, we can zoom out for a second and look at this question for what it really is. Someone is offering you a drink. Humans beings drink. We need water and countless other H2O based beverages to survive. You're being offered a drink and I recommend you take a beverage without alcohol. There has never been a time in history with more alcohol-free beverage options. My advice—accept the offer and go with a soda water with a splash of cranberry, which is the best drink ever. You can also have fun with this question. Some of my favorite responses are "No thanks, you don't have nearly enough alcohol here." Or, "No way, this body is a temple." Or "Would you like a drink, Paul?" "Let me take a look at your homeowners policy first…" Lighten up and have fun with this question.

Saddle up

- ☐ Do you find yourself rehearsing ways to decline a drink?
- ☐ How do you respond when offered a drink?
- ☐ What responses do you get when you decline a drink?
- ☐ Stand in front of a mirror and practice saying no to a drink. Look yourself in the eyes. Don't forget to remind yourself why you're declining the drinks. Make sure this comes from a place of compassion and hope for a better future and not out of fear.
- ☐ What are some fun and creative ways you can say no to a drink? Start a collection. Have fun. Lighten up.

A.A.—Alcoholics Anonymous

In 1934, just after Prohibition ended, a troubled stockbroker named Bill Wilson landed himself in a hospital in New York City. Rumor has it, Wilson drank close to a half-gallon of whiskey a day, which he tried to stop several times. He was given a plant medicine called Belladonna, which at the time was being used as an experimental treatment for addiction. It is said that in his hospital bed, he verbally called out for God to loosen his grip on alcohol and he reported seeing a flash of light and feeling serenity he had never felt before. Bill W., as he's known, never had a drink of alcohol again and the following year in 1935, he co-founded Alcoholics Anonymous, with Dr. Bob Smith, more commonly known as Dr. Bob.

At the time, A.A. filled a vacuum in the western medical world which offered relatively few answers for alcoholism. When tuberculosis was cured in 1934, tuberculosis units emptied, providing ample space to treat alcoholism under the direction of the program Alcoholics Anonymous. As A.A. grew, many of these vacant spaces were converted into alcoholism wards, and this is where many new members were recruited. Since, apart from the detoxification process, western medicine yielded unfavorable results with addiction, and A.A. took this problem off their hands. Thus, the separation of western medicine and addiction began.

In my opinion, Bill W. and Dr. Bob got a lot right when they created A.A., and they didn't have the luxury of building off other programs because they were the first. For the most part, they hit a home run from the start. A.A. was a big part of what propelled me forward in my AF life. I went to over 100 meetings in my first 90 AF days and got an incredible sponsor who walked me through the steps. We met at a coffee shop every week for nearly a year and I'll forever be thankful for his unconditional generosity and support.

Now, of course the program isn't perfect, and I do feel that if they don't change their stances on a few things in the future, mostly in regard to anonymity, the program may find their numbers shrinking. Studies show that although the number of people struggling with an alcohol addiction is on the rise, the population of A.A. remains stagnant. If members of A.A. keep up with this steadfast anonymity, people who are ready to ditch the booze may join programs that are less anonymous and have marketing teams. One of the main goals of Recovery Elevator is to shred the shame, to start a dialogue around addiction in hopes of destigmatizing addiction, and this isn't far off from what A.A. founder Bill W. had in mind as well. Below is an excerpt from *As Bill Sees It*.

> *As a rule, the average newcomer wanted his family to know immediately what he was trying to do. He also wanted to tell others who had tried to help him—his doctor, his minister, and close friends. As he gained confidence, he felt it right to explain his new way of life to his employer and business associates. When opportunities to be helpful came along, he found he could easily talk about A.A. to almost anyone. These disclosures helped him to lose his fear of the alcoholic stigma and spread the news of A.A.'s existence in his community. Many a new man and woman came to A.A. because of such conversations.*

It sounds like Bill W. originally intended for A.A. members to burn some ships, but somewhere along the line, a stricter curtain of anonymity was drawn for members to stand comfortably behind.

In 2008, I went to Las Vegas with my dad, brother and several other father/son combos for a cigar convention. I was a passenger on the addiction struggle bus that trip and I remember feeling like a complete loser because I couldn't control my drinking. I found out a couple years later that there was someone in recovery on that trip, but I had no idea, despite sitting across from this guy at a couple dinners, that he didn't drink. He was supposed to be anonymous. If we don't talk about this, the rate of addiction may climb faster than the word of recovery can spread.

One thing to keep in mind is that A.A., for the most part, only addresses the pain at the end of the addiction cycle and not at the start. In 1935, knowledge of how unresolved past traumas can lead to addictive behaviors later in life and an understanding of the human brain were in their infancy and I feel that if the program were created today, much space would be dedicated towards addressing past emotional pains, neglect, suffering and trauma.

A.A. worked for me and countless others but it's not for everyone and the success rates aren't as high as you'd think. The debate over the efficacy of 12 Step programs has been quietly beginning to surface over the past decades among addictionologists and has sped up with the passage of the Affordable Care Act. A.A. is difficult to study by its way of creation. It keeps no records of who attends meetings; members come and go and are of course anonymous. In 2006, the Cochrane Collaboration, a healthcare research group, reviewed studies going back to the 1960s and found that "no experimental studies unequivocally demonstrated the effectiveness of A.A. or 12 Step approaches for reducing alcohol dependence or problems." *The Big Book* included a segment in the second edition which was published in 1955 that states: A.A. has worked for 75% of people who have "really tried." It says that 50% got sober right away and another 25% struggled for a while, but eventually recovered. These figures are based on members' experiences according to A.A. In the book, *The Sober Truth*, Lance Dodes looked at Alcoholics Anonymous's retention rates along with studies on sobriety and rates of active involvement (attending meetings regularly and working the program) among A.A. members. Based on his findings, he puts A.A.'s actual success rate somewhere between five and eight percent. I personally don't know if I would be sober today without A.A., and find this statement hard to believe, but I feel if I want to fully cover alcoholism and treatments, this needs to be included. In fact, even if it is an eight percent success rate, that's damn good considering it's $1 per meeting and the success rates of 30K+ month-long treatment facilities are only a few percentage points higher.

If you're wondering how to get a sponsor, there's no magic to it and all you have to do is ask. Wait till you hear someone you resonate with, walk up to them after the meeting, turn off the thinking mind, and say, "Will you be my sponsor?" There is no need to overthink this process.

Contrary to popular belief, A.A. isn't a religious program, despite having a direct or indirect reference to GOD in seven of the twelve steps, but rather a spiritual program that invites you to navel gaze with the guidance of someone who has already walked the path you're embarking upon. Again, this GOD is clarified countless times in *The Big Book* as a God of your understanding and isn't the guy on the cross. I see way too many egos never giving the program a chance (and this was me in 2013), because they feel it isn't in line with their religious ideologies. Let me say this again, A.A. isn't a religious program, but a spiritual one. Russell Brand does a great job of demystifying A.A. in his book *Recovery* and breaks down the steps to the modern-day equivalent of "It's time to unfuck yourself and here's how."

I also hate hearing the argument saying "I don't want to attend A.A. because I might see someone I know." Think about that one for a second. Normal drinkers such as your boss, your neighbor, and your daughter's 5th grade teacher don't attend these meeting with the goal of uncovering who in their city has a drinking problem. If you do see someone you know, they have the same goal of being the best version of themself and it looks like you two have something huge in common. Walk up and say "Hello."

I do HIGHLY recommend giving A.A. a shot. This is the easiest way to develop an in-person community of other like-minded individuals. Don't write the program off after a couple meetings because there is such a variety of meetings. If you live in a city big enough, check out at least 10-15 meetings in different areas of town. Each meeting has its own vibrational frequency and keep scouting them out until you find one that energetically feels right.

Saddle up

☐ What do you think about A.A.? Have you attended a meeting?

☐ Have you found yourself saying, "A.A. won't work for me because it's a religious program, or I don't believe in God?"

☐ If you haven't attended an A.A. meeting, make it a goal to attend 5 different meetings in the next thirty days.

Meditation and Mindfulness

"Meditation. There is nothing to do. It is about undoing."

—Dzogchen Ponlop Rinpoche

This is a big one. Stop thinking, and start being. Most people think meditation involves sitting on a cushion, with hands on knees while repeating "ohm" (ohm is the sound you get when you combine all known sounds in the universe). Sure, this is one way to do it, but it's important to keep in mind that there are infinite ways to meditate, and it's more important to understand the 'why' of meditation than the 'how' of meditating. In his book *Life Visioning*, Michael Bernard Beckwith states, "it's not what meditation is, because that's the ego getting into the "how to" loop and not focusing on what is meditation which is giving undivided attention to the universal truths of this moment." When we slow our brain waves down, we can enter the operating system of the brain and begin to change the future. Meditating is about weakening the energetic bonds with the past and future and we do this each and every time we bring our attention to the present moment. Siddhartha Gautama, who got the kickass nickname Buddha, said that "all we are is the result of what we have thought," and through meditation, we have the ability to let unconscious false narratives dissolve and evaporate.

Your consciousness can focus on anything, even itself. Instead of being aware of the constant drumming of thoughts, try becoming aware of consciousness itself. We are always thinking about something, but this time we are thinking about the source of consciousness. The holy grail of meditation is focusing consciousness back towards consciousness. A good way to do this is to take 4-5 deep, controlled breaths and then hand over the task of breathing to the body. As you do this, try to focus on the moment when your body, which contains a vast divine intelligence, takes over breathing.

During meditation it's important to be vulnerable. There are fragmented parts held deep within the unconscious mind and it's important to let them surface on their own time. In order to initiate the internal healing, things need to freely surface from any time of our life, be it good, bad, sad and joyful and it's important to keep in mind we can't expedite this process by seeking out uncomfortable unconscious thoughts but rather let them surface when ready. Do your absolute best, and keep in mind this is a practice (takes practice) to remain open when an uncomfortable thought or emotion arises. These thoughts are minuscule subatomic energetic particles that the body is trying to release and it's important to let this natural healing process happen. It's important that we let all these energetic patterns go—both good and bad.

When we explore the riverbanks of our emotions and allow this energy to be released from the body it can get scary, mostly because we begin to enter the unknown which is void of certainty, routines and identities. Not wanting to go here is natural, but you must. In the unfuck yourself journey to overcome addiction, eventually this is where your path will lead you. As my man Eckhart Tolle says, "being at ease with not knowing is crucial for answers to come to you." The mind will fight, it will protest, it will dig its heels into the mud and say, "Nope, not happening," but this is where you and your heart must go. I'm not asking you to do anything I haven't done nor something I won't do again in the future. Eventually you will start to understand there is nothing in the deep recesses of your body and in the unknown of the future that can harm you.

According to Dr. Joe Dispenza, author of *Becoming Supernatural*, "Quantum science demonstrates how, through meditation, when we enter the unknown, the mind can truly signal new genes to behave in new ways, down-regulate unhealthy genes, access stem cells in the body, and create new healthy cells in the body where cells have been damaged. This means you're not doomed to express whatever genes you've inherited, and you can literally rewrite your mental and physical future states with meditation."

Meditation isn't about acquiring or getting anything, it's quite the opposite. True liberation arrives from letting go of all thoughts—including the happy ones. Eventually, we wizen up and recognize we don't want any of this stuff kept inside but flowing steadily and beautifully through us. It's important that we start letting go now because there will only be more stuff to let go of later. Here is some great news; a powerful source of fuel for this journey isn't derived from accumulating anything, yet a substantial amount of power is derived from letting go.

Through meditation we start to recognize the present moment is infinitely more important than any moment in the past or future. After all, if we were to play a song on the piano, we don't play the song just for the last note.

There's growing evidence that mindfulness, which is an intense focus on the present moment and can be done at any moment of the day, can counter the dopamine flood of contemporary life. Researchers at the University of Washington (Go Dawgs, I went to grad school there) showed that a program based on mindfulness was more effective in relapse prevention than 12 Step programs.

When we go through life in a state of mindfulness, less labeling takes place. For example, the next time you look at a pine tree, do your best to view it as living organism and not something with a label or name. If you do this long enough, you should start to witness the colors in nature becoming more vibrant and energetic. You'll begin to perceive without thought.

The only way to mess up a meditation is to skip it. There is no such thing as an unsuccessful mediation as long as you do the practice, even if your thoughts pull you in all directions for the duration of the practice. I'll be honest, meditation is hard work. In the beginning it takes discipline but within time, your mediation practice will become tolerable, and then enjoyable. As I mentioned, there are endless ways to meditate, but I recommend starting off with guided mediations from apps like HeadSpace, Calm, The Mindfulness app and Buddhify. I had a paid membership to the Headspace meditation app my first two years AF and it helped immensely. Nowadays, I meditate 3-4 times per week, 10-25 minutes, in the morning or evening and it has become one of the most enjoyable parts of my day. In addition, I perform several mini meditations throughout the day. For example, I have taken several one to two conscious meditative breaths while writing this section.

In May of 2019, I attended a 5 ½ day silent meditation retreat that rocked my world. In addition to over 30 hours of meditation, there was no talking, internet, music, reading, or smartphone, for over 130 straight hours. My holy goodness, there were a lot of firsts. Halfway through day three, I could see and feel the ego, the false created self, start to dissolve, which was both liberating and terrifying at the same time. The question of "who am I" without all the external reinforcements is constantly being challenged but ironically, we get further to the truth of who we truly are when the identities and roles the false self has created begin to weaken. I would highly recommend attending a meditation or even a silent meditation retreat. It was one of the most profound inner journeys I've ever gone through and I'm hoping to do more, perhaps even longer, silent retreats in the future.

A successful journey into an AF life is all about action, and ironically, a big action item is to stop doing. I recognized early in this journey that I labored to be still. I could barely sit through an hour-long A.A. meeting, was always fidgeting and had to get up and walk around. The thought of entering a float tank in early sobriety would have put me into a ball of anxiety. Today, sitting is one of my favorite activities. There's a park bench on a hill about five minutes from my office and when it's 45 degrees or above, my dog Ben and I probably log four to five hours per week on this bench. As the philosopher Nietzsche wrote in a rare moment of deep stillness, "For happiness, how little suffices for happiness!"

Saddle up

- ☐ Do you have a mediation practice? How you do meditate?

- ☐ Meditate for 20 minutes. Get comfortable and breathe in for four seconds and breathe out for four seconds. Do your best to let all thoughts go and return your focus to the breath.

- ☐ Find a comfortable place outside to sit. Be mindful of your surroundings. Observe the weather, the trees, the smells and how you're feeling.

The Why

This is where the journey, once again, can get confusing. Alcohol isn't the problem. Drinking is the result of internal unease… alcohol is used to dull emotional discomfort, trauma, neglect and other painful life experiences. The first time I heard this, I was like "Bullshit, I drink because I like how it makes me feel." Although this statement is true, as I progressed in my AF journey, it became evident I was using alcohol to mask feelings of alienation and loneliness…and that my heart had crumbled into a million little pieces after leaving my first love in Spain at the age of 21. Oh yea, the rock band I was in broke up that same summer. I was drinking in the short term to cover up an accumulation of long-term pain, and for me this was always loneliness, shame and guilt. In all reality, it isn't a question of "Do I have a drinking problem?" but, "What am I using alcohol to cover up?"

If you don't know where to start when it comes to addressing the why, don't worry—once you quit drinking, you'll start to find out and the body will always give you clues. You can see this when emotions aren't in line with a situation. For example, if you've experienced abandonment in life, you may become overly agitated when someone is only a few minutes late to pick you up. Or if a statement from a stranger has the ability to send you into a complete tailspin, this is another indicator of a preconditioned emotional response based on past experience. We spend years covering up this discomfort with alcohol, so when it is removed the body fast-tracks the 'why' to the surface and this can be extremely uncomfortable. It is important to embrace these feelings as teachers and opportunities to heal. If we manage to become AF and the "why" isn't addressed, then ultimately, we begin to swap addictions and the internal unease remains. Bessel Van Der Kolk, M.D., in his book *The Body Keeps the Score*, says "As long as you keep secrets and suppress information, you are fundamentally at war with yourself."

According to Kymberly Stephens, LPC and Certified Expert Trauma Professional, unresolved trauma is typically stored in the right hemisphere of the brain, which oversees intuition and emotions. Instead of being encoded chronologically, trauma memories are stored experientially from what the person heard, saw, felt, and smelled. Therefore, many of our trauma memories show up in our day-to-day functioning as symptoms. These symptoms can include depression, anxiety, feeling numb or on edge, decreased concentration, insomnia, mistrust, and self-harm. If the trauma is not addressed, then these symptoms will continue to surface and can trigger the beginning of a new addictive or destructive pattern of coping.

Most people don't confront the 'why' in early sobriety and that's okay. I know I didn't. Removing alcohol can be enough of a shock on the system. Don't go looking for the 'why'. The body will let you know when and where to begin and as your awareness builds, the why should start to reveal itself. As Nadine Burke Harris says in her book *The Deepest Well: Healing Long-Term Effects of Childhood Adversity*, "This might sound simple, but I cannot overstate this: the single most important thing is recognizing what the problem is in the first place."

The best way to transmute the 'why', or these intense recurring emotional charges, is to sit with it and anchor yourself by mentally pulling all your energies back to the body. The instant an uncomfortable energetic front presents itself, locate it in the body and send all your awareness to it. If you're at work or in public, try to find a place where you can be alone for a couple minutes. Once you've pinpointed where these units of past mental energy live, squeeze and hug this region with awareness. Close your eyes, place all your focus into this region and breathe into the area. To compound this, squeeze the muscle that would stop urination mid-stream and slightly flex your lower abdominals while inhaling. This internal friction you're creating with the breath helps expedite the process of releasing stored energy. With this technique, in a matter of months, I was able to pull the anxiety that I felt in my solar plexus my entire life into my heart region where it's met with warmth and love. My anxiety levels have dramatically decreased with this technique.

Don't ask for the removal of the emotion but breathe into it and allow it to be. Doing this allows the tumultuous sea of emotions to pacify, and the next time this energetic charge is triggered, it will be much less intense until the emotional charge has completely dissolved.

Saddle up

☐ What do you think the 'why' is behind your drinking? Write down all past traumas you've experienced in life and if you think you've processed or dealt with these situations. Think of things that perhaps didn't happen in your life. For example, you didn't receive the emotional support you needed from a family member as a child.

☐ Since you've removed alcohol from your life, has the 'why' started to emerge?

☐ Have you noticed any preconditioned emotional responses that aren't in line with a situation? What are they?

Depression, Anxiety and Stress

Depression is a bitch, anxiety is the worst, and stress can wreak havoc on quality of life. However, as the Sufi mystic Rumi said, "These pains you feel are messengers. Listen to them." I used alcohol to muffle these messengers until no amount of Cuervo could quiet them, and I had to listen. The message was loud and clear. Quit drinking and stop living in the past and future. Depression is when mental energies are stuck in the past, anxiety is when we are living in the future, and stress accumulates when an end goal is more important than the task at hand. What the mind can't see and will dedicate countless units of mental energy toward the past and future seeking a solution, is that liberation from all three of these dysfunctions resides in the present moment. In addition, the mind, the ego, will do everything in its power to avoid the present moment because its identity is sourced from the past and future.

There is an undeniable connection between alcohol and depression; after all, alcohol is a depressant. The bulk of melancholy should lift, as was my experience, after the removal of alcohol within a matter of months. However, if depression lingers, a couple things might be happening. Part of your identity at the unconscious level is someone who is comfortable being unhappy, and the thought of a happy life and the unknown is uncomfortable. Another reason is that you're constantly dwelling in the past looking for ways that situations could have been handled differently in hopes of a better future. It's prudent to access the past to make better decisions in the present, but if we are always living in the past, and the past consists of depression, then the future has already been written. If you are still experiencing depression in your AF life, don't worry—again, there is nothing fundamentally wrong with you. Direct your mental energy into the present moment. You may have to repeat the process a couple thousand times, but eventually, you'll get the hang of it and the depression will begin to lift.

Anxiety levels, too, should return to baseline after removing alcohol. In a 1991 study, researchers tested 171 hospitalized males with an alcohol use disorder (AUD), forty percent of whom reported significant anxiety on admission. When questioned about their psychological state, they perceived themselves as chronically prone to anxiety and described their drinking as a means of self-medicating their discomfort. After two weeks of abstinence, however, their anxiety levels returned to normal. At a three-month follow-up, anxiety had declined further. For those who relapsed, anxiety shot back up again.

Anxiety, which always has a relation with a future event, is the absolute worst, especially after bouts of heavy drinking, and was the primary driver for my decision to quit drinking. After a couple months AF, about 90% of my anxiety had disappeared. Thank goodness. However, there was still a persistent underlying anxiety that lingered around. For myself, and I know I'm not unique with this, anxiety has always signaled three things: 1. I'm mentally living in the future 2. My identity, according to the ego, at some future moment is challenged and 3. I'm excited. These days, for the most part, the anxiety I feel, and it's important not to incorrectly label this as bad, is a sense of excitement.

If you are feeling anxious, regardless of what stage you're at in an AF life, it's important to recognize that you're not alone and you're not fundamentally flawed. Anxiety rates among the general population are at an all-time high according to the National Institute of Mental Health. This jittery mood has given rise to what Rebecca Jennings at Vox has dubbed "anxiety consumerism" which shows up in the rise of products from fidget spinners, essential oil sprays, weighted blankets and perhaps the most popular item in this category: alcohol. This new class of product represents a growing unease on the planet. In unprecedented numbers, people more than ever are starting to listen to their anxiety, which is why more people than ever are exploring an AF life. People are starting to wizen up and realize alcohol may be the culprit and not the cure to anxiety.

Just as we did with feelings of depression, if you find yourself anxious, take a seat, fill the belly with breath, and pull yourself back into the present moment.

When we are primarily focused on an outcome, and not on the task at hand, we experience the accumulation of stress which can be devasting to the equanimity in the body. When we perform daily tasks at work and home only as the means to an end, or when all attention is placed on a future goal or identity and not on what currently needs to be accomplished, stress will inevitably build. Stress always has an inverse relationship with presence. If you're in a stressful period in life, most likely the ego has attached happiness to a future event which strips away any possibility of enjoying the tasks required to achieve this goal. Right about now seems like a good time to insert the famous Ralph Waldo Emerson quote, "Life is a journey, not a destination."

Saddle up

☐ Do you think depression, anxiety and stress are here to tell us something? To signal change? Are they messengers?

☐ When you're feeling depressed, do you find yourself thinking primarily in the past? When feeling anxious, are thoughts directed towards the future?

☐ Do you think you may find comfort in depression or states of anxiety because it's the known and familiar?

☐ Do you think you've incorrectly labeled anxiety? Could it be excitement?

☐ Do you think true liberation from depression, stress and anxiety resides in the present moment?

☐ Why do you think it's so hard to stay centered in the present? Can you see the protective personality/ego constantly pulling you back to the past or future?

Fear

I'm sure you're hoping this book contains the magical formula to eliminate all fear in life. It doesn't, but I've learned how to work with it, as opposed to fighting it. The primary coping strategy I used for over thirty years to deal with fear was the acronym FEAR: Fuck Everything And Run, which yielded pitiful results, which is why I've developed a much better technique that I'm excited to share with you.

Everyone experiences fear (except that crazy guy Alex Honnold who free climbed Yosemite's El Capitan without ropes) and ultimately, it all stems from the fear of death. Fear can be split into a bunch of mini deaths in life when we feel we're going to lose something such as an identity, a reputation, financial resources, routines, and friends to name a few. The presence of fear is a good indication that the protective personality is calling the shots and there is a feeling we don't have enough resources to survive. Fear is a lack of trust… However, just as addictions are signposts in life, fears are also messengers indicating underdeveloped parts of the body that need special love and attention. One would be mistaken to think we conquer fear, that would be fighting darkness with darkness, but instead we work with it, listen to what it's trying to tell us and compassionately bring these areas up to speed on the new life direction. This is what I want you to do the next time you feel fear creeping up in every cell of your body. This action item is critical because all parts of the soul need to be on the same page. Find a quiet, safe place and take a seat. In your mind, slowly walk towards these fears with an open posture and sit. Let them know, in a neutral voice, you will no longer be ignoring them and you're there to listen. Perhaps in this mental scene, bring your favorite pet or a dear friend that can hang out in the background if needed. Ask your fears if there is anything they'd like to say, and then repeat back to them what you hear. If you don't fully understand what the fear is telling you, that's okay, simply being with them is what's important. Ask your fears what fears they have and if there is anything you can do to soothe the suffering of your fears. Maybe ask your fears if they'd like to watch your favorite show on Netflix with you, then have a seat on the couch, pop some popcorn and get to know each other.

The next time you find yourself in a scary dream or nightmare, do your best to stay in the dream. In dreams, you've got a direct connection to the unconscious mind. No matter how terrifying it may be, turn around, hold your footing and say hello to the fear. You'll find that big scary monster isn't as scary as you thought and is seeking the same thing as you: love and acceptance.

I know this exercise may sound strange, but I've had to do some form of this exercise every morning while writing this book. I'd be lying if I said fear was absent while writing this book. One morning, I asked my fears what they were trying to tell me, and I was surprised by the response. One would think fear levels would diminish the more chapters I complete, but this wasn't the case, which spiked my curiosity. Before I began writing one morning, I sat with my fears, and simply asked, "Why is fear rising as I near the completion of the book?" As I quieted the mind, I remembered a home video of me playing soccer when I was five years old. I would sprint past the other players, and then run in place directly in front the ball. You could hear my dad and other parents saying, "Paul, kick the ball." "Why isn't he kicking the ball?" And then it hit me. "Holy shit!" I blurted out. I've been afraid to kick the ball in life and writing this book is helping me lean into those fears. It doesn't matter if this book sells 1 million copies or keeps a barrel fire lit at the local homeless shelter, this is me worrying less about what could go wrong and more about what can go right. Not kicking the ball and taking a chance in life was comfortable, I knew what to expect. That chapter in life is coming to an end. I'm entering the unknown, and so are you. Let's do this together.

Saddle up

☐ What does it feel like in your body when you experience fear? When does fear arrive? Is it tied to a certain place or circumstance?

☐ Ask yourself if you think everyone experiences fear. Do you think fear can be healthy? Is it telling you what to run from, or is it telling you where to go?

☐ Write down your current strategies of how you deal with fear. Write down some new strategies you'd like to explore.

☐ Write down what you think fear has been holding you back from doing? How much does fear control your life? If fear wasn't part of your life, what do you think your life would look like?

☐ The next time you feel fear building, lean into it and start befriending the fear. Ask the fear what it's trying to tell you and what direction it wants you to go.

Diet & Exercise

At six months AF, I read the book *All Day Energy Diet*, by Yuri Elkaim and made close to twenty small changes in my diet and fitness routine. This, coupled with removing alcohol from my diet, resulted in a tremendous boost in my physical and mental wellbeing. I found taking 10mg of L-Glutamine daily in my first couple months away from alcohol helped with cravings and healing the gut. Research shows this amino acid can reduce both cravings and the anxiety that accompanies alcohol withdrawal. L-Glutamine also helps with sugar cravings which is beneficial since alcohol is loaded with this other addictive substance. Sometimes we mistake our cravings as alcohol cravings when the body is screaming for sugar. I also loaded up on B vitamins (B-100 and B-Complex) during the first six months since alcohol abuse can deplete vitamin B. I took milk thistle the first three months to help stimulate the regeneration of liver cells. At nighttime I took 200 mg of L-Theanine, which can naturally be found in green tea, to promote relaxation and calm before bedtime.

Adding vital nutrients and supplements to the body should improve your wellbeing, but keep in mind, headaches, and inflammation in the body aren't caused by a lack of Aspirin in the system. As you deepen with the concepts and strategies mentioned in this book, physical healing should happen naturally. I don't recommend placing too much emphasis on finding the perfect cocktail of nutrients, vitamins, amino acids, minerals, enzymes, oils, and tinctures. If you remove the toxin alcohol, add compassion in your life, lighten up, quiet the mind, then the body will find itself in a harmonious environment conducive to physical healing.

Since diet and exercise isn't my area of expertise, I won't be recommending a specific plan, but I encourage readers to dedicate time and energy to this arena.

Some people lose weight when they remove alcohol from their diet while others, as you're adding vital, previously absent, vitamins and nutrients into your diet, gain weight. It's important to trust the body, which has millions of years of experience built into its genetic code, and let the healing happen.

It's completely fine if shedding some extra pounds is part of your motivation to quit drinking, but I want you to shift your goal from losing weight to being the best version of you. For example, before you go for a walk or run, instead of saying I'm doing this to lose weight, tell yourself you're doing it to take your body for a walk because you love yourself and want to be the best version of you. Don't crush kale smoothies out of fear of becoming overweight, but because you want to feed your incredible body with healthy fuel. Don't intermittent fast in hopes of ridding yourself of unwanted toxins, but because you cherish the body and want to give important digestive systems a rest. Make these dietary and fitness changes not out of fear but to deepen with your wholeness.

Be careful with "addiction whackamole" and don't replace drinking with exercise. Exercise is a much healthier alternative to drinking, but it's important that we don't literally "run" or "jog "ourselves into another addiction.

I highly recommend the meditative, physical and spiritual practice of yoga which does wonders for mental health, reduces inflammation throughout the body, and improves respiration, energy, and vitality, to name just a few. It is rumored that yoga is the gateway drug to spirituality.

A great way to stack strategies covered in this chapter is to work out with others who don't drink. You can build an alcohol-free community, hold yourself accountable and exercise. Do a google search for "yoga for recovery" to see if there are classes in your area geared towards those who want to ditch the booze.

While implementing a new exercise plan, start slow so you can build confidence and enjoy it. Maybe run a ½ mile the first week, then ¾ mile the next week and then 1 mile for the next month.

Saddle up

☐ Was part of the motivation to quit drinking losing weight? If so, try to rewrite the narrative and tell yourself you won't be drinking because you want to be the best version of you.

☐ Before exercising or preparing a healthy meal, be sure to reinforce you're doing it out of love for yourself and your physical body.

☐ Try a new exercise routine. Join a fitness class. Hire a personal trainer and do some yoga.

NICE JOB! Over the past two chapters, we covered a boatload of concepts and some killer strategies that will give you the confidence, insight and internal power to ditch the poison called alcohol. I recommend revisiting these past two chapters regularly throughout your journey as the scales from unconsciousness to consciousness begin to tip more towards your favor. Some of these strategies may be a shock to the system early in an AF life.

Be patient and gentle with yourself. Some strategies might not resonate with you in your first year or two AF and that's completely fine. Some of them might not ever be part of your unfuck yourself portfolio, and that's also fine. I know that for myself, I wasn't ready to dive into meditation until a couple years after taking my last drink. There are countless action items in these past two chapters, that I WANT you to explore. I'll be the first to admit, simply reading this book won't do much without incorporating these tools into your life. I want you to saddle up. You can think all day about your dream house, but until you get a hammer and nails, it's never going to be built. In a fast-paced world, you'll need to make concessions with your time and make this journey a priority. Of course, you'd rather binge-watch *The Sopranos* instead of sitting toe to toe with your fears, but this is what needs to happen. Gone are the days we pull joy and happiness from the future for short term pleasure.

Take a look at the past two chapters at the end of your day. If you had a challenging part of a day, or the whole day was a mess, it's more than likely that you were given several opportunities to implement one or more of these strategies. Once your intention to quit drinking has been heard by the universe, scenarios where you can practice these concepts will start to show up. Of course, some of these strategies are scary and confusing to explore at first, but within time, they will become second nature and resorting to alcohol to overcome life challenges will be a thing of the past.

Keep in mind, this isn't the complete playbook to an AF life. I'm a firm believer there are infinite ways to successfully depart from alcohol; I also don't believe moderately consuming alcohol is part of the equation. Listen to the body. It will always, without fail, tell you where to direct your awareness and where to go next.

Chapter 11
A Cure to Addiction

"You might need to ditch the booze if...your friend buys you your own plastic wine glass because you've broken so many of hers while drunk."

—Angie, Atlanta, GA

A cure to addiction...is this possible? Can western or eastern medicine bail us out of one of the most prolific health crises of our time? In the early 21st century, scientists, modern medicine, psychologists, psychiatrists, and other medical professionals are still desperately trying to figure out effective treatments, let alone a cure and regrettably, I don't think one exists—especially in tablet form. The reason is that overall, addiction isn't something that is cured, but prevented, and I'm optimistic that humanity will get its shit together, start living harmoniously with its own species, the planet, its inhabitants and inner turmoil that leads to addiction will decrease. Currently, addiction is on the rise but I'm hopeful this will reach a climax in the near future and that generations to come won't face addiction like we are seeing today. Millennials get a lot of flak, but they might be on to something as this is the first generation that hasn't fully subscribed to the mainstream norms and are doing things differently. They are taking gap years (yes, plural) after high school, taking longer to graduate college, most likely will move back home with the nuclear family sometime in their adult lives, don't care about getting driver's licenses, won't work a minute over 40 hours per week, are taking their first sips of alcohol at a later date and are drinking less overall than previous generations. Good for them. They might be the first group to collectively wake up and realize that the "American

Dream" needs more month-long vacations, road trips, avocado toast and fewer mortgages.

Now, currently, although there isn't a cure, I want to be clear that countless individuals have successfully said goodbye to alcohol and other substances to go on to lead happy and fulfilling lives. I'm walking proof of this and have met thousands who have done the same. I'm a firm believer we can fully rebound from any addiction using the concepts and strategies I have invited you to explore in this book.

So how will addiction become obsolete? How does the internal connection remain intact so that a person doesn't have that pull to soothe inner discomfort with an external substance or behavior? Well, let's put on our imagination hats and take a look. Hang with me for a second. Keep in mind that this is all speculative, and some of these ideas may seem farfetched, but if we take a step back and look at the trajectory of the human race, this is where we are headed. Some of you will agree, and some won't. Who knows, if this book is still in circulation 500 years from now, I may have nailed it, or wildly missed the mark. History shows that for millennia we have been on a trend toward unification as a species.

Before we imagine the future, let's take a quick look at the past. In my opinion, the most profound line in *The Realm of Hungry Ghosts* by Dr. Gabor Mate, is that anthropologists have no record of addiction in pre-modern times. Contrary to popular belief, European explorers were not the first to introduce alcohol to the native populations in the Americas, the Inuits in the north, and the Aborigines in Australia. Alcohol has been around for thousands of years across the globe and records show many of these cultures routinely used the "spirit" alcohol in rituals and in life. So why is it that only within the past 400-500 years has abuse of alcohol and addiction been such a problem? Why has the swath of addiction caused more havoc within some groups more than others?

There has never been a time in history where so many people have been displaced or dislocated from their lands in such a short time frame as there is now, and some cultures have taken the brunt of it. Prior to a couple hundred years ago, things didn't change much, for generations.

Today, when we have the "When I was a kid…" talk, the listener is often completely baffled and has trouble imagining a way of life that existed just 25 years ago. I lived the first 12 years of my life without internet and was tethered to a phone with a cord (ironically, we were more free when the phone was connected with a cord). Today, we suffer from what psychologists call the paradox of choice, which is that the more choices we have, the less satisfied we become. We are constantly pinged with products that promise happiness and then find ourselves confused when it doesn't happen. Social media feeds tell us we need to make at least a six-figure income, remodel another floor onto the house, run a daily 10k, be perpetually happy and it's all bullshit. The inauthenticity of social media is a plague to modern society. Even more ironically, Mark Zuckerberg will be remembered as the guy who both connected and disconnected the world.

However, people are starting to wake up to this nonsense and say, "Wait a second, I was told if I climbed the corporate ladder, bought a log cabin in the Yellowstone Club and owned several jet skis, I would be successful, but it doesn't feel right. I'm not happy." Currently, we are a culture living in a wobble because the definition of what happiness and success look like are completely fucked. These growing pains are necessary for us to depart from a society that is addicted to consumerism, wealth, vanity, and alcohol to name a few. There is a growing consciousness on the planet that is starting to recognize the absurdity of our current path, and you are part of this collective waking up. On a global scale, people are starting to say, "Time out, hold the phone, it's time to hit the pause button. That formula that I was told to follow in life isn't yielding the fruits I was promised."

Okay, back to the cure to addiction, or I should more accurately say, how to arrive at an environment that cultivates wholeness. I was at my annual fantasy football league draft this past August in Las Vegas. While eating at the Hofbrauhaus, I was watching my friend Sean argue with my buddy Pete about immigration. They have had this same or a similar pointless conversation the past five fantasy football drafts and although I knew a resolution wasn't going to be reached, I still listened. As they were defending their steadfast positions with volleys based partly on fact but mostly on conviction, a peculiar thought arrived. A voice inside my head muttered, "The only way to solve immigration is to get rid of borders." Como? What was that? I was surprised by the sudden thought that arrived and I couldn't get rid of it. I then stepped outside the restaurant, into the stifling hot Vegas night and started connecting the dots until I said to myself, "Holy shit, that's the cure to addiction."

There have been short chapters of isolationism throughout history, and we're seeing some of that now with Brexit and the attempts to build a wall on the southern U.S. border, but according to Yuval Noah Harari in his book *Sapiens*, human beings are headed in a direction of unity and have been for several thousand years. I'll be honest: although a world without borders as John Lennon alludes to in his song "Imagine" sounds like a nifty idea, it's still uncomfortable to sit with, even though we've been moving forward in this direction for quite some time now.

Let's take a moment to explore a futuristic world without borders. The human ego has been doing the divide, conquer, defeat, overthrow, coup, rebellion, revolution, wage war, WWI, WWII, with sticks and clubs and now with nuclear bombs for millennia in hopes of claiming land and spreading ideologies to create a utopia that has yet to arrive. This approach consistently puts the "heaven on earth" at a future date and humans are starting to wizen up and recognize this promised paradise is unattainable with this tactic. Human beings on the planet are more open than ever to a different strategy and we're starting to see some unlikely characters in political positions for this reason. Never before in history have we seen so clearly the limitations of external power within such a context for change. The insatiable conquest for more land, wealth, fame and power, which only delivers short term satisfaction at the expense of others is coming to an end. We are collectively beginning to explore the currency of inner peace that is infinitely more valuable.

In 1985, the Schengen Agreement was passed by the European Union, abolishing checkpoints and bringing Europe to the main stage. The internet has demolished borders that denied access to information for billions across the globe. Barring a full-on nuclear holocaust, radical global heating or artificial intelligence getting out of hand, a world without borders could happen in the next 300-500 years; or around when we all have the same beautiful skin tone.

In the meantime, we don't need to wait for governments to start actively working towards this goal, and in fact, the cultivation of a society that promotes wholeness has to start within. To circle back to the internal versus external concept, we first need to become aware of the borders we have constructed within ourselves and work towards opening the heart, mind and body. If, on an individual level, we work on dissolving the internal walls and barriers we've built up throughout life, then our society as a whole will inevitably open up as well. It isn't your job to solve all of the problems on the planet, but it is your duty to recognize the lessons this compassionate universe has placed before you and heal the parts of you that most need healing.

If all of us 7.5 billion souls on the planet stop pointing the finger at the speck in the other person's eye and work on removing the plank in our own eye (yep, just dropped a Bible quote) then the inadequacies of the external world—hatred, resentments, shame, guilt, envy, despair, depression, anxiety, doubt, and addiction (which can all be seen for what they are: borders) will dissolve in time.

How will we know we're on the right track? It won't be a sheet of paper where we check off boxes when physical borders are eliminated. The barometer of success into a world free of addiction will be joy. It will not, and cannot, be a grueling fight. Waging war to eradicate borders won't work either. We'll know we are on the right track when this road to a more loving planet becomes easier. As the internal disconnection mends, this process will become easier as hearts and minds soften. On the flip side, we'll know we've derailed when we see an influx of new products into the anxiety consumerism market and addiction continues to rise. When we start to widen the flow of love into our life then joy, which feels like a baby penguin is taking a nap on your heart, will become the more consistent emotional state. We will become less materialistic and place more value on the infinite currencies of gratitude, empathy, compassion and joy. Joy is not something to be captured but cultivated.

Joy is like a wild animal that will only make an appearance if the conditions are right. If you run around blasting negative thoughts and energy in your life, then there should be little surprise if joy is absent.

When everyone can move about this planet freely, when we can accept all human beings as equal, when we are able to establish roots and communities wherever we'd like, then we'll start to see the epidemic of addiction fade. You have heard me say the three most dangerous words we can say on this journey are "I got this." That puts us on a lonely island where it's just I, and maybe a coconut or two. But on the flip side, I know with all my heart, "we got this." Together, collectively, we will all heal from our addictions in one of the most beautifully orchestrated collaborative efforts mankind will ever see. We are just beginning this monumental healing that everyone and everything will take part of. It will be the most remarkable time for all living species on the planet and we're about to blast off. Get ready. I want you to be part of it.

Chapter 12
Trust

"You might need to ditch the booze if...you keep extra beers hidden in the garage to secretly replenish the bottles in the house, so it doesn't look like you've drank that much."

—Russel, Woodinville, WA

Great job! We've covered several concepts and strategies that will propel us forward in a happy, joyous, alcohol-free life. You've tuned the gaze inward which takes a tremendous amount of courage. I'm proud of you, and you should be too. I think that about covers it… Wait, there's one more thing I almost forgot. Oops, my bad. It's a big one because this is what we lean into when we begin to detach from the thinking mind and enter the unknown. No, this isn't where the book takes a religious turn but it is where I invite you to explore trusting that something, apart from you, has your back, that every life situation you've experienced has happened for your benefit and we don't have to figure out every detail in life. This concept, that I simply call "trust," allows us to chill out and recognize we don't have to make everything happen in life, and that in fact, the majority of it unfolds regardless. Again, this "trust" thing doesn't have religious underpinnings. It may for some, but it's about recognition, and I think we can all agree that there is way more happening than meets the eye. In fact, quantum science has proven that humans can see only 3-4% of what is actually in front of our eyes.

We are probably a dozen Einsteins away from figuring out what the point of our existence is and why we're floating around in an infinite universe on a spaceship without a roof, but until then—if it ever happens—I ask you to lighten up, and trust in whatever created the most incredible miracle of all time: you. We have reached a unique crossroads in history where science and spirituality are starting to speak the same language. Quantum science has discovered that separation is the biggest illusion of all, and that everything is connected. We are all created from the same space dust and are all one. This is fantastic news since disconnection is the main culprit of addiction.

Did you know water responds directly to our thoughts and words? In the mid 1990s Dr. Masaru Emoto, a Japanese scientist set out to see if thoughts, ideas, and music could have any effect on water. Dr. Emoto's method involved showing words to the water, playing music to the water and praying to the water. After that, he froze the water and then observed the frozen crystals in the microscope. What he found astonished him. The frozen water crystals that were showered with love, froze in harmonious, beautiful patterns while water that was exposed to negative thoughts and hatred froze in ugly fragmented shards.

Another example of this interdependence, that we are all connected, is the study done by Dr. Cleve Baxter, the author of *Primary Perception*. He had the idea of hooking up a plant to a polygraph machine to see if plants could read our thoughts. He assumed that the plant would exhibit a constant flat electrical pattern regardless of what he was thinking about the plant but was amazed when this wasn't the case. To test this, he set out to invoke a fear response in a plant. The plant was hooked up to the machine for 14 minutes before he had the idea to go get a match to burn a leaf. Before Dr. Baxter, who was seated 16 feet from the plant, could even stand up to get the match, he noticed the plant experiencing some serious distress. The plant didn't calm down until Baxter relinquished the malicious thought of burning the plant. This study, which has been replicated many times, shows that plants are conscious and can detect the energetic vibrations that are coupled with our thoughts.

This next one completely boggles the mind. In David Wilcox's book, *The Sourcefield Investigations*, he explores a scientifically controlled study done in 1978 with a group of 7,000 expert meditators. The group meditated together for a period of three weeks focusing on thoughts of love and peace. Shockingly, it was found that during this same three-week timeframe, there was a 16% drop in crime on a global scale, suicides and car accidents also dropped and, global terrorism dropped by 72% during this three-week period. Researchers and scientists were even more astonished when they ruled out possible variables such as weather, holidays, global events and anything else that could have caused such a decline. There was nothing in particular that was different during this three-week period, except there were seven thousand meditators sending love and world peace throughout the planet. Similar studies have been repeated hundreds of times with the same results.

Crazy stuff eh? Whether you believe in Jesus, Allah, Buddha or a Chia Pet, I encourage you to deepen with the idea that you don't have to figure it all out; including your relationship with alcohol. It's important to have the "why" you'd like to move forward in an AF life clearly defined, but don't worry about the "how" because the universe will solve that one for you once you're ready to put the bottle down. Once you've set the clear intention that you no longer want alcohol in your life, then a compassionate universe will work with you, not against you, to help you reach this goal. Quantum science is proving that once your intention, or goal is clearly defined, your external environment will synergistically start to align for the realization of what you have asked for. In short, what you seek is also seeking you. Once clearly defined and set forth into the universe, no intentions go unanswered.

This where Newton's first law of motion comes into play, which states that every object will remain in motion (in this case, it's an addiction) unless compelled to change its state by the action of an external force. The key point here is that if there is no net force acting on an addiction, then it will move forward unchecked. Once the case for "why" you want to quit drinking has been made throughout the body and the conscious and unconscious mind, then the "how" will start showing up from a higher consciousness that also wants you to ditch the booze. This opposite net force can look like uncomfortable emotions, anxiety, depression, headaches, job loss, physical accidents, DUIs etc. The forces acting against the addiction in the external environment will always match the loss of control and turmoil in the internal environment.

I'm not making an interesting analogy; this is actually what is happening. Trust that something out there is working in tandem, alongside you, at all times during this journey.

What you'll eventually find when you lean into trust, is you have a tremendous amount of energy that doesn't come from food, water, sleep, exercise, alcohol, prescriptions or drugs. In ancient Chinese medicine, this is called Chi. In Yoga, it's called Shakti, and, in the west, it's called spirit. Call it whatever you want, it's important we lean into this infinite source of energy as we move into an AF life. The most important requirement to building this "trust" muscle is to relax, resist nothing, pick up your oars, and go with the natural flow of life. The consciousness that created the human cell—which measures one thousandth of an inch across and contains enough data in its DNA to fill a 600,000-page book—is on your team and has nothing but the best wishes for you. At times, it may seem like your current life situation doesn't make any sense, but it will.

Building trust takes time and I recommend going slowly with it. At times, this can be scary. It may feel as if you're standing at the edge of a cliff. When you lean into trust, you'll begin to realize your previous definitions of who you are, or who you've become, no longer hold the weight they used to. This is both liberating and frightening. You'll know you've entered the waters of trust when you begin to recognize that the mind-created self, the protective personality, the ego, was all a fabrication of the mind, and that you, or the construct the mind created, doesn't exist. Once this begins, a magical thing starts to happen. You'll begin to stop thinking and start being. This is the most important action item of the book. Stop the incessant mind chatter and start enjoying this beautiful thing called life. All of it. People are constantly thinking and implementing elaborate ways to change a life situation, but we never end up feeling much different. Hit the stop button on this hedonic treadmill and get off. Everything that's needed to be joyous in life, we already have. The mind will be eager to disagree with this statement, but the heart knows it's true.

As you begin to deepen with trust, you'll realize that little to nothing in your external environment needs to change, that everything is fine just the way it is. If and when change does occur in your external world, it will mirror the growth and shedding of old skins in your internal environment. Limiting beliefs that you've had your entire life begin to dissolve, freeing up space for joy to enter. You'll start to realize that all beliefs are limiting and that anything is possible in an alcohol-free life. In the introduction, I mention this book has a beginning and an end, but they aren't found in the customary locations. The beginning of this book represents the end of your old life that is no longer serving you, and here we are at the end of the book, which is the beginning of your new life. Now start being.

Saddle up

☐ Do you think a greater consciousness is working with you, in your favor?

☐ Can you begin to trust that a greater order is working in your favor?

☐ Do you think your intention to depart from alcohol has been heard?

☐ Ask yourself if you think the repercussions of your drinking match the level of your addiction.

☐ Place more energy on the "why" you're quitting drinking and less on the "how."

☐ What are the things you'd like to accomplish in a life without alcohol?

☐ What are some limiting beliefs you have towards yourself?

☐ Start being the person you were always intended to be.

Last Call

Don't forget, alcohol is shit. To end, here are some more useful guidelines indicating that you may need to ditch the booze…

"You might need to ditch the booze if…"

If you do your recycling at 3 a.m. so no one will see you.

—Ricky, Durham, NC

If a friend calls you who you think you haven't heard from in a long time, only to realize they are calling you back because you called them the night before in a blackout.

—Rachelle, Portland, OR

If you have a budget line for "Alcohol" and "Alcohol-related" transactions...

—Greg, Edmonton, AB

If you buy a pint of vodka that you take two shots of and pour the rest down the sink and then head to a different liquor store about an hour later to buy another pint of vodka that you dump mostly down the sink because you are "moderating."

—Lauren, Chattanooga, TN

If you still find full/empty/half empty bottles 6+ months into being sober!

—Michael, Rockton, IL

If you're in junior high school and you steal wine from your parents and stash it in a Mrs. Butterworth syrup bottle in your bedroom closet.

—Darla, Grand Junction, CO

If you only order top shelf for your first drink, and the cheap stuff the rest of the night since you'll hardly remember it anyway.

—Chris, OR

If you strategize for the week where you're going to be buying your booze as you don't want any one place to think you're drinking as much as you know you are.

—Tom, Bentleigh, VIC

If you're so drunk you leave yourself a voicemail while trying to get someone to come pick you up from the bars...and your face drops the next day when listening to voicemail because you called yourself, realizing that's why you had to take a cab.

—Katie, Arlington, TX

If you promise to quit drinking for the month of January, then realize college football isn't finished, so you push it to February.

—Tim, Fullerton, CA

If the guy sitting next you on the plane gets up to use the bathroom and you chug his Heineken before he gets back because the flight attendants had already cut you off!

—Meghan, Epping, NH

If you keep a case of wine in the garage and six bottles in the wine rack and one bottle in the vegetable drawer...but only you know there's also a box of wine...just in case.

—Patty, Corvallis, OR

If you switch to drinking liquor because beer makes you full so you can't drink as much.

—Tiffany, Westminster, MD

If your friends invite you to pre-party before a night out, and you've already been pre-partying on your own.

—Chris, OR

If the cashier at the liquor store already has your bottle ready before you even come in.

—Michael, Rockton, IL

If you wake up on a cruise ship in your friend's room and the closet doors are ripped off the hinges and carefully placed leaning against the wall like they belong.

—Kirby, Charleston, SC

If you trick different doctors into giving multiple prescriptions because you know your destroying your liver, but you want to keep drinking.

—David, Nuevo, CA

If you wake up in a pub in London in a back room after they have closed… at 2:00 p.m. the next day.

—Barry, Huntly, VA

If you have to refer to dozens of nights by the kind of beverages consumed—'the night with all the sake bombs', 'the night we drank that whiskey with the rattlesnake in it', 'the night we were drinking out of the giant glass boots', etc.

—Christopher, Washington, DC

If you factor in the calorie intake of alcohol into your calorie-controlled diet.

—Craig, Denny, FAL, UK

If you take secret shots from a freezer bottle at your ex/ baby daddy's house, and you realize the bottle is getting too low and you're worried he'll notice...so you have to replace it ...but pour off enough out of the new bottle into a Tupperware in your car so you can replace it stealthily.

—Katie, Arlington, TX

If all the pictures that you are tagged in on Facebook are at wineries, breweries and speakeasies.

—Rachel, Minneapolis, MN

If you don't want to look like a sad gal drinking alone, so you buy a round of drinks for the newlyweds eating in the bar area...sing a song to them...and ya don't even know them!

—Denise, Littleton, CO

If you make up elaborate stories about the people that are coming over to drink with you (to cover why you are buying so much alcohol at 10 a.m.), only to, in reality you go home to watch Netflix with your dog.

—Jonathan, Gilbert, AZ

If you buy a round of shots for your friends at the bar, then drink them all before they get back from the bathroom.

—Andrew, Shreveport, LA

If you have three blood alcohol calculator apps on your phone in hopes of preventing blackouts.

—Lucy, Watford, HRT

If you've probably spent more than $400 paying off Mexican police officers from the stupid shit you've done while drunk.

—Paul, Bozeman MT

If your dad is taking your liquor and replacing it with water…in high school.

—Kirby, Charleston, SC

If you get up in the middle of the night after a bender, are dying of thirst and chug what you think is a bottle of water-only to discover it's hydrogen peroxide. My hubby had to call poison control right after I did it. They asked, "Is she throwing up yet?" He said "No," and the lady on the other end of the line said "Well, she will." Big time. Get ready.

—Melissa, Brookfield, IL

If you throw away your corkscrew because you never want to drink again and have to buy another one…over and over and over.

—Suzanne, Pell City, AL

If you make your work schedule around your hangovers.

—Jonathan, Gilbert, AZ

If you replace the ice water in your Starbucks cup with Moscato while in the underground parking lot before returning to work after lunch.

—Lindsay, Vacaville, CA

You pass out at a concert, while in the first row and don't wake up until it's over.

—Diane, Nuevo, CA

If you're pretending to cook with a bottle of wine at your in-laws just so you can down the entire thing in secret to deal with them.

—Rose, Dijon, FR

If you can open a bottle of wine with a steak knife or a screwdriver.

—Suzanne, Pell City, AL

If you live by yourself and hide your empties from yourself so you don't have to be reminded of how much you drank the night before.

—Sherina, Amityville, NY

If you have the alcohol contents of the microbrews memorized at your favorite brewery.

—Ben, Amarillo, TX

If you hide your bottle under the couch and it clinks the other empty bottles that you forgot that you've hidden.

—Rachel, Minneapolis, MN

If the only thing in your purse at your cousin's DRY wedding is nips.

—Emily, Roanoke Rapids, NC

If your roommate calls the cops on you to end your parties.

—Paul, Bozeman, MT

If you 'come to' in a jail cell, next to Superman, an elephant, and a scary clown and have no idea how you got there...the day after Halloween.

—Kerri, Redding, CA

If you decorate your wine bottles as fun Christmas decor.

—Lauren, Chattanooga, TN

If you drink a six pack before meeting up with friends.

—Jonathan, Gilbert, AZ

If you start drinking wine out of a mug so the neighbors think you're just having a cup of tea.

—Rose, Dijon, FR

If you're like Norm from Cheers because everyone at your favorite bar knows your name.

—Denise, Littleton, CO

If you graffiti your OWN bathroom wall while in a blackout. I woke up to "keep your fork, there's pie" scrawled above the toilet paper dispenser.

—Elaine, Burnaby, BC

If you're yelling at people to buy you more wine when you can't even walk.

—Kim, Sacramento, CA

If you've puked and rallied… three times in one night.

—Drew, Reno NV

If you remember people by what they drink, but forget their names.

—Faye, Chapel Hill, NC

If you go to a bar and when they ask to see your I.D., you hand them a calculator… access denied.

—Betsy, Belmont, NH

If when you go to the liquor store to buy alcohol for the week, the cashier asks you if you are hosting a party. #partyofOne

—Rachel, Minneapolis, MN

If you've been in a book club for 2.5 years and have yet to read a book, because all we do is drink.

—Erin, Bakersfield, CA

If the reason to leave the house, is to buy more booze, but you tell your husband that your friend Ericka needs help organizing her closet.

—Katie, Tulsa, OK

If you almost go to Mexican jail because you ran naked past a wedding party having a romantic dinner on the beach to skinny dip in the ocean after tequila shots at an all-inclusive resort in Playa del Carmen.

—Angie, Atlanta, GA

If you walk next door to your neighbor's house with your favorite glass full of wine and she says "I have a flower vase exactly like that."

—Joy, San Diego, CA

If you can't find your car keys so you punch a hole through the windshield to get in.

—Beth, Beverly, MA

If 99% of your "Facebook memories" involve a picture of you with a bottle in your hand.

—Rose, Dijon, FR

If you "threw in the towel" during a field sobriety test, then forgot about it, then was reminded when the officer played his recording in a hearing. My Lawyer wasn't happy about that.

—Bill, Albuquerque, NM

If the next day after a bender, the find my iPhone feature shows your phone in the middle of a sewage plant.

—Brady, Huntsville, AL

If on a first date you chug a beer while she is in the bathroom hoping you can get the second one ordered and delivered without her knowing.

—Russell, Grand Rapids, MI

If you wake up in the morning with a bed full of chips and salsa, including a mouthful that you were eating when you passed out the night before.

—Jen, Pittsburgh, PA.

If you sit on your best friend's bridal shower cake.

—Meredith, Ipswich, MA

If while doing puzzles drunk, you think you're on a hot streak, only to find the next day most of them are mashed together and the puzzle is ruined.

—Paul, Bozeman, MT

If you keep hiding empty vodka shot bottles inside a boot in your closet until no more will fit.

—Diane, Nuevo, CA

If you draw dash marks on your wrist to see how many drinks you had before blacking out.

—Emily, Roanoke Rapids, NC

If you repeatedly find yourself befriending and drinking with homeless people because they're the only ones up and drinking at 4am when all your friends have gone home.

—Lucy, Watford, HRT

If you pass out on an ant hill while camping.

—Paul, Bozeman, MT

If you wake up after a blackout while camping and find yourself crawling up the bank of a lake and then spend the next few hours scrambling through the bush in the middle of the night until you stumble onto a road.

—James, Port Macquarie, NSW, AU

If you spend 8 hours in the swim up bar at your brother in law's bachelor party.

—Brad, Fort Wayne, IN

If you blackout and leave yourself notes around the house informing you of the previous night's events.

—David, Mulberry, FL

If you're packing for a move (drunk) and put your passport "somewhere safe." You can remember the somewhere safe thinking line but not WHERE you put it. And then find it 3 years later between two framed photographs you never hung back up.

—Katie, Passaic, NJ

If you've had 4 new phones in a 3-month period because you keep losing them at the bar.

—Adam, Atlanta, GA

If your surgery is cancelled because you thought that not drinking anything for 12 hours before surgery meant not drinking alcohol.

—Jeff, San Francisco, CA

If you had to see your favorite band 5 times because you don't remember the first 4 times.

—Nadine, Colorado Springs, CO

If you take a giant drink of whiskey, throw up in your mouth, swallow the throw up, then keep hitting the bottle!

—Scott, Denver, CO

If you don't buy any beer with less than 8% alcohol.

—Brandon, Peoria, IL

If you're always the last person standing at the party.

—Rose, Dijon, FR

If you go to pee in the middle of the night and realize you missed the toilet by an entire room.

—Darren, Oshkosh, WI

If at 500 days sober, you're still finding empty beer cans and bottles in your house.

—Alvin, Santa FE, NM

You have fake conversations on the phone in a liquor store and say things like, "Yeah Mike, I'll pick that up for ya, wait, you want that bottle also?"

—Jason, Sheridan, WY

If the guy at the liquor store offers you a 10% discount because you come in so often.

—Tyrrell, Bozeman, MT

Acknowledgements

First off, I want to thank alcohol—yep, even though you nearly took my soul and life. Without you, I wouldn't have the incredible life I have today. Thank you, alcohol, for showing me where I need to go in life and where I definitely don't want to go. I hope we never become reacquainted again but thank you for giving me the courage to look within, face my fears, and make profound changes in my life. You have been the best of teachers.

Thank you to my mom Molly, my dad Perry, and my brother Mark. There is no chance this book happens without the unconditional love from the Churchill family. Mom, thank you for always being my ultimate cheerleader in life. Perry, I'm sorry I refilled your 18-year-old Scotch Whisky with Black Velvet...73 times. Mark, thanks for dropping everything and flying out to Montana after my night in the suicide-proof jail cell.

To Ben the giant poodle—you saved my life. Thank you infinity times.

There are countless who helped make this book a reality. There is no way to include everyone and everything, but I want to express my gratitude to these people, places, entities, ideas and things for making this project happen. Brady, Sean, Pete, Paul E., TJ, Jesse, Dusty (the best sober sidekick a guy could ask for), Daryl, Bob, Brandon, Donny, Ben, Andrew, Collette, Kaz, Noah P., Brandon B., MT Netters rec hockey team, Coach Taylor (Alta Hawks), Joe, Pat, Abe, Dan, Tim, Laura H., Britany H., Morgan N., Maria L., Amber, Mr. Phelan, Professor Dockett, A.A., Ayahuasca, my editor and resilience coach Lorca Smetana, Kerri Paniagua-Smith (has been my office manager for the past three years and was sent from above), podcast editor Tyrrell Lourie (another angel sent from above), Kellie Ideson, all the members in Café RE and the courageous sobriety warriors I've met while doing Recovery Elevator, all those who have attended a Recovery Elevator retreat, meet-up or sober travel trip, the Peru Crew, La Croix Soda Water, my podcasting mic, all the sponsors for the podcast, Sarje Haynes, Buddy, Romualdo (was my business partner in Spain and I can only imagine what it was like to run a bar with me), Ruben, Fernando, Martin, Dave, Johannes, Marcos, Sana, Sofia, Edouard, Matthew, Adam, Mawine, Charly, Chapman University, Peruvian Hearts, Papi's Treks, Pete Sveen, Dustin Rising, Andrew Youderian, Pat Haggarty, Bryan Walthall and the Wednesday morning business mastermind group, THIRD EYE BLIND, water, the reader who wishes I could write better than an 8th grader, planet earth, Gerry and the wonderful staff at Rythmia, tapas, Elaine Huang with Embodiment of Freedom LLC, Odette Cressler with the Harmony Tribe, Tricia Lewis with Recovery Happy Hour aka, the Unicorn of Sobriety, Shane Ramer, Omar Pinto, Reece's Pieces, all the maple donuts my first year AF, the lessons learned while going 0-10 playing football at Battle Mountain High School, this compassionate universe, howler monkeys in Costa Rica who had my back, the skillset I was given, the present moment, my intuition, Romee, Spanish Creek mountain range and all the trails I hiked my first 30 days AF, skeeball, my kickball team Denim Venom, all the people who I've had soul contracts with, Eckhart Tolle, Annie Grace, Gabor Mate, Michael Bernard Beckwith, Gary Zukov, Mark Manson, Nine Inch Nails, Coldplay, Hope Rehab in Thailand, Randy R, Kathy V, Kerri MacFarlane, Mike N., Madeleine Y., sunlight, Patrick W., Ponderosa Pines, Yoga, Anam Thubten and the Dharmata Foundation, Dr. Sue Morter, Dr. Michael Steward, Kymberly Stephens, Dr. Joe Dispenza, Yuval Noah Harari, Ziad Masri, Pema Chodron, The Dao De Jing, Kris O., Michael Pollan, Michael A. Singer, Katherine Ketcham, Pat Flynn, John Lee Dumas, Sarah Hepolah, Bill Wilson, Dr. Bob, the recovery community in Bozeman, Montana, Anne Lamott, and the critic.

Thank you to everyone who has been courageous enough to burn the ships and share your story. Every time someone comes forward about how alcohol didn't deliver what was promised, the narrative around the slippery and elusive drug alcohol begins to change and others become empowered. Thank you to those who burned the ships before me and gave me strength to do the same.

Thank you to everyone who helped save my life.

Reach out:
https://www.recoveryelevator.com
info@recoveryelevator.com
Instagram @recoveryelevator

About the Author

In 2006, at age 23, Paul Churchill moved to Granada, Spain, where he purchased a bar. During the following three years he became addicted to alcohol, blacking out close to seven nights a week. In 2009, Paul walked away from the bar hoping a geographical cure would curtail the drinking but he continued to drink for another five years until he took his last drink on September 6th, 2014.

In February 2015 Paul launched the Recovery Elevator Podcast as an accountability tool to quit drinking. Today, the podcast has surpassed 3 million downloads, is in the 95th percentile of all podcasts on iTunes and has been downloaded in all 50 states and over 145 countries.

Paul currently lives in Bozeman, Montana and loves to get outside and hike with his sober sidekick Standard Poodle Ben. In the wintertime, he does his best not to injure himself while playing ice hockey.

THANK YOU
FOR READING
ALCOHOL IS SH!T

It's time to start shredding the shame and start talking about this. If you've decided to remove alcohol from your life, be proud of this decision and let others know. If you've enjoyed this book, please leave a review on Amazon, share it with someone who may be struggling with alcohol and invite normal drinkers to read this book as well.

For more information about Recovery Elevator, the podcast, the private community Café RE, the free 5 day video course, upcoming events, retreats and sober travel trips, visit:

https://www.recoveryelevator.com
Be sure to follow Recovery Elevator on
Instagram @recoveryelevator

Thoughts and comments? We'd love to hear from you.
Email us at info@recoveryelevator.com

Don't forget, the most badass thing about you is that you don't drink!

Made in the USA
Monee, IL
07 November 2023

45957185R00129